Art Bead
JEWELRY

Seasons in Glass

by Karen Leonardo

KB
KALMBACH BOOKS

Kalmbach Books
21027 Crossroads Circle
Waukesha, Wisconsin 53186
www.Kalmbach.com/books

Published in 2009
13 12 11 10 09   1 2 3 4 5

Manufactured in the United States of America

ISBN: 978-0-87116-280-9

Publisher's Cataloging-in-Publication Data

Leonardo, Karen J.
   Art bead jewelry : seasons in glass / by Karen Leonardo.

   p. : col. ill. ; cm.

   ISBN: 978-0-87116-280-9

1. Beadwork--Handbooks, manuals, etc. 2. Beadwork--Patterns. 3. Jewelry making--Handbooks, manuals, etc. 4. Glass beads. I. Title. II. Title: Jewelry

TT860 .L466 2009
745.594/2

CONTENTS

INTRODUCTION 4
ABOUT LAMPWORKED BEADS 5
DESIGNING QUALITY JEWELRY 12
JEWELRY-MAKING BASICS 17

THINK SPRING.................................. 22
Easter Parade Necklace..................................... 23
Steel Magnolia Choker....................................... 26
Tulsa Spring Garden Set..................................... 28
Flower Chain Mail Necklace 33
Frog Eggs Necklace 38
"Think Green" Silver Clay Core Bead 42

SUNNY SUMMERTIME 44
Under the Sea Bracelet 45
Do You Know the Way to San José? Necklace 47
Incan Queen Bracelet 50
Chunky Cheer Bracelet 53
Sweet Treats Charm Bracelet & Earrings 56
Treasure Island Necklace.................................... 60

BRISK AUTUMN 65

Teahouse Necklace............................... 66

Fall Ribbons Necklace 68

Tribal Princess Necklace 71

Autumn Sunset Necklace...................... 76

Run for the Roses Necklace 80

WHISPERING WINTER........................... 85

Sleigh Bells Necklace 86

Snowflake Dazzle Ring 88

Crisp Winter Days Necklace................. 91

Smoky Indigo Choker 94

THE CLASSICS 98

Black & White Opera Earrings............... 99

Coco Elegance Necklace...................... 101

Royal Kimono Necklace and Earrings.............. 104

Wildly Sophisticated Bangle 107

LAMPWORK AND JEWELRY ARTIST DIRECTORY................................. 110

DEDICATION, ACKNOWLEDGMENTS, AND ABOUT THE AUTHOR..................... 111

"CELEBRATE EVERY SEASON IN STYLE WITH JEWELRY DESIGNED AROUND GORGEOUS LAMPWORKED BEADS."

INTRODUCTION

Lampworked glass beads bring joy to the wearer and pride to the collector—their popularity has grown among collectors and jewelry designers alike. Each lampworked bead is special and adds a classic touch to your jewelry designs. Since it is made by hand, each bead is truly one of a kind! This book will tell you about lampworked beads and show you how to choose, purchase, and clean your lampworked beads. You will learn more about lampwork and how to use these special beads to make gorgeous jewelry. You will learn to use lampworked beads with gemstones, silver, gold, seed beads, wire, jump rings, and more.

Each jewelry project has complete instructions and detailed step-by-step photos. Learn how to stitch a spiral rope for the spring Frog Eggs Necklace (p. 38), or make a classic design with a sparkling

Coco Elegance Necklace (p. 101). Create a cute Sweet Treats Charm Bracelet (p. 56) for a summer night, or whip up a Teahouse Necklace (p. 66) for a crisp fall day. Browse through the pages and make whatever catches your eye. The beads in this book are all made by talented artists, but you can substitute similar beads for your own jewelry.

I can't wait to show you all of these gorgeous jewelry designs. Let's bead!

Karen F. Leonardo

Each project in this book lists a Skill Level. Simple projects that require only a few stringing or wire-working techniques are listed as Level 1. Projects that use more techniques are listed at Level 2. The most challenging projects in the book are listed as Level 3.

Begin with an easy project if you have little jewelry-making experience. Once you have practiced your skills, you can try some of the more challenging projects.

SKILL
LEVEL 1

SKILL
LEVEL 2

SKILL
LEVEL 3

ABOUT LAMPWORKED BEADS

The most important element of lampworked beaded jewelry is, of course, the lampworked bead. It is the focus point of the design, whether used in a set or as a lovely focal. First, let's discuss what lampworked beads are. I will give you reasons why you should use lampworked beads in your jewelry designs and take you through the process of making a lampworked bead. We'll also discuss what qualities to look for in a bead.

WHAT ARE LAMPWORKED BEADS?

Lampworked beads are handmade glass beads created by using a torch. To make a bead, an artist first heats a glass rod and then winds the molten glass around a mandrel. A mandrel is a steel wire or rod of varying thicknesses; it is coated with a bead release, or flux, that allows the bead maker to remove the bead after it cools. The beads can be as simple as a single-color round or as intricate as a miniature painting. The hot glass can be shaped into almost anything, as long as it has a hole so it can be strung into a piece of jewelry.

Necklace by Debbie Weaver

THE HISTORY OF LAMPWORKED BEADS

Lampworked beads go back thousands of years, when artists made their beads over special lanterns or candles. However, we don't know exactly when lampworking began. Hot glass techniques began around 1700 BC with the Syrians, but the Romans and Italians were probably the first bead makers to use the ancient processes of glass to make a bead. The Italians jealously guarded their glass "secrets" for many years, and their basic techniques are still used today, only with more technical knowledge, innovative torches, and precise flames. The contemporary lampwork movement has been growing in leaps and bounds over the last 20 years or more. You can now buy glass from all over the world in many different colors and types, and lampwork classes are available throughout the North America and abroad. Beads and special lampwork techniques and processes are now being documented. Bead museums all over the world now preserve lampworked bead history.

WHY USE LAMPWORKED BEADS?

If you want your jewelry to have an extra-special touch and custom look, you will want to use artisan handmade lampworked beads. Each bead is unique. You can find a focal bead that has all the colors you just love and design your jewelry piece around the focal, or you can purchase a nice set of lampworked beads that goes perfectly with the gemstones that have been sitting on your work table.

Some artists develop their own unique styles or become well-known for their special techniques and tools. These tools allow the artists to expand their creativity. You may enjoy a particular artist's style and develop a jewelry line directly from his or her beads. Many lampwork artists will custom-make the beads you've been craving for a truly personal look.

Bead by
Karen Leonardo

ABOUT GLASS

There are two types of glass beads: those made with hard glass (borosilicate, also known as boro) and soft glass.

Soft glass rods

Hard glass rods

The difference between these two glasses is in the temperature at which they melt and their degree of hardness (the Coefficient of Expansion, or C.O.E.). The lower the C.O.E., the harder the glass. Soft glass has a 90–104 C.O.E., and hard glass is around 32 C.O.E.

In addition, glass comes in different colors that range from basic to metallic or opalescent. The color palettes for the two types of glass vary; some shades are not available in soft glass.

Leonardo Imprint tools

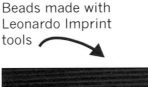

Beads made with Leonardo Imprint tools

Making a
SIMPLE GLASS BEAD

The process of making a bead starts with a torch, glass rods, mandrels, and a kiln. It's also important to use special eyeglasses to protect your eyes. The following is a basic description of lampworking; for more details, consult a lampworking book or tutorial.

1 Dip your mandrels in bead release and set aside to dry.

2 When the mandrels are dry, turn on your torch. Heat a glass rod in the flame until the end of the rod melts.

3 Heat your mandrel. Touch the tip of the hot glass to the mandrel and wrap the hot glass, making a round-shaped bead.

4 Evenly heat the bead in the upper part of the flame (this process is called *flame annealing*). Then slowly cool the bead in a kiln.

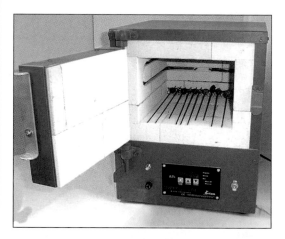

Dot Party 3 by Marianne Filaggi

Examples of
BEAD SHAPES

Sculpted bead
Bead by Anne Dunsmore

Sculpted flower beads
Beads by Karen Leonardo

Bicone bead
Bead by Karen Leonardo

Disc beads
Beads by Karen Leonardo

Lentil focal
Bead by Karen Leonardo

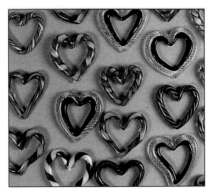

Shaped pendants
Beads by Mike "Fig" Mangiafico

Hollow bicone bead
Bead by Karen Leonardo

WHAT MAKES A GOOD BEAD?

First of all, you should like what you are buying. Remember, beauty is in the eye of the beholder. Make sure there are no jagged edges on the bead or around the hole that could cut your beading wire or catch on clothing. The placement and size of the hole should allow the bead to lie properly and not flip around or become top-heavy in a design. Lastly, check for any errant air bubbles that could crack and mar the design. Other than these simple requirements, your choice of bead is up to you!

CHOOSING APPROPRIATE BEADS

When designing jewelry, you will want your beads to be wearable. Quality jewelry is durable and comfortable. If you are making bracelets or rings with your beads, be aware that they will get more wear and tear than earrings or necklaces. Don't use sculpted flowers or beads with fragile projections unless you are extremely careful with your jewelry; these types of beads are fragile and better suited for necklaces or earrings. Solid beads without protrusions are great for bracelets. Rings also receive a lot of punishment from everyday wear, and it may be best to wear them just for special occasions.

Petal earrings by FIG

Bead suited for jewelry by FIG

Snowflake Dazzle Ring (p. 88)

Bead suited more for collection than jewelry by FIG

PURCHASING LAMPWORKED BEADS

You can buy lampworked beads directly from a bead artist's Web site or from auction sites, bead stores, magazines, and shows. Search for beads on the Internet or look for advertisements in bead magazines. Check your local newspaper for special bead shows coming to your area. Prices will vary depending on the skill and popularity of the glass bead artist.

CARING FOR LAMPWORKED BEADS

Treat lampworked beads with care. Store them separately in plastic bead boxes, wrap them in tissue and stack them, or purchase specially made bead displays.

Lampworked bead storage box

Clean your beads before using them, if needed. Carefully wash glass beads with soap and water, polish with a cotton cloth, or brush with a fine brush. If dust accumulates in the tiny crevices on a bead, use a soft toothbrush to brush the dust out of the corners.

Be careful not to brush too hard, or you may break off fine pieces. If pieces break off too easily, you may not have a high-quality bead. Some beads are more fragile than others and should be treated with more care. If you drop beads, whether sculpted or round, on a hard surface, expect them to crack or break, and count your blessings if they don't. If the bead hole needs to be cleaned out better to remove powder residue, take a bead hole cleaner (purchased at your craft store) and ream out the inside. You may also use a pipe cleaner.

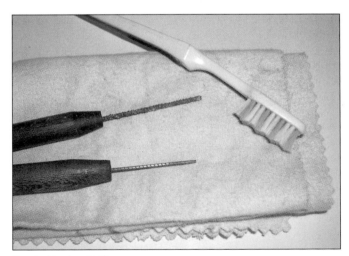

Bead cleaning tools

DESIGNING QUALITY JEWELRY

Design by Leslie Jones, beads by
Karen Leonardo

Design by Leslie Jones, beads by
Jennifer Cook

Each of us prefers certain colors and styles of jewelry—that is what makes us special! Your unique style reflects who you are. You may like bold, exotic lampworked jewelry that shouts, "Look at me!," while someone else may prefer a small lampworked pendant on a chain.

Let's talk about how to design your jewelry with lampworked beads using the elements of design, personal style, and color. Good jewelry design incorporates wearability, weight and size, balance, durability, and security. Wearability is the most important aspect of the jewelry piece. It takes all the other factors into account. The weight and size of a piece should be comfortable and suit the wearer. The weight of earrings should not pull on earlobes, and bracelets should not have any edges that snag on clothing. Necklaces should not be too heavy or require the wearer to make a trip to the chiropractor!

Be sure your bracelets lie comfortably on the wrist. You may not want to use delicate or fragile beads, as bracelets endure a lot of wear. If desired, use hard glass beads in bracelet designs for added durability.

Balance allows the jewelry piece to lie properly. If a piece is off-balance, it will be uncomfortable and require constant adjustments. Asymmetrical designs are difficult to balance, but they are very attractive when crafted properly. The materials used in your design should be durable, long-lasting, strong, easy to maintain, and well-made. Always use quality findings to secure your jewelry.

DESIGN PRINCIPLES

Many principles of design can be at work when you create a piece of jewelry: balance, repetition, contrast, harmony, and others. Some pieces will flow from just one or two of these principles. Sometimes many will be at work in one piece. As you develop your "designer's eye," these concepts will become second nature. Here are some illustrations of the principles at work in jewelry.

Contrast in scale, texture, or color, as shown here, keeps the eye moving across a piece.

Black & White Opera Earrings, p. 99

Symmetrical balance, or symmetry: Equal components rest on either side of the focal.

Bead by Kim Miles, design by Teri Sallwasser

Asymmetry: The balance in the piece doesn't rely on symmetry, but on other elements, such as color, weight, or repetition. This is where your designer's eye really comes into play!

Tribal Princess Necklace, p. 71

Size contrast: One component should not be too big or small compared to the rest of the piece.

People Bead Necklace by Laurie Salopek

Emphasis means stressing a particular element within the design, which helps determine a focal point for the piece. In this piece, the artist emphasized the face by adding hair fibers and placing the bead in a silver circle. This design also emphasizes the bead and draws the viewer to the bead's eyes.

Bead and necklace by Debbie Weaver

Harmony is a sense of oneness, achieved by using similar textures, lines, shapes, and colors. All the components should come together to make a pleasing design.

Lampwork by Jennifer Cook, design by Teri Sallwasser

Variety: An assortment of design components adds more interest to the piece.

Beads by Karen Leonardo, design by Cindy Vela

FOCUS ON THE BEADS

When designing with lampworked beads, take into account what suits you and what attracts you most. Do you want to work with focal lampworked beads or sets of beads? What sizes do you want to wear? Some beads also have elements to work with (for example, spirals or geometric lines). What are your favorite colors and shapes? Do you like encased floral beads, or do you prefer sculpted flowers? When you find the perfect lampworked bead to create a jewelry piece, decide what the best design would be based on the bead's size and shape. Consider the colors in the lampwork, and choose which bead colors you want to emphasize.

COLOR

Color brings individuality and creativity to our world. Without color, our world would be listless, boring, and mundane.

HUE, VALUE, AND CHROMA

Color is measured by hue, value, and chroma. *Hue* is the combination of shades on the color wheel that contain the same colors. For example, yellow-orange is closer to the yellow family than orange-yellow, yet both hues contain the same colors. *Value* refers to the lightness or darkness of a color. *Chroma* refers to the intensity of a color. Colors with weak chroma are dull, while colors with strong chroma are brilliant and bright.

PRIMARY, SECONDARY, AND TERTIARY COLORS

Colors can be either primary, secondary, or tertiary. Red, yellow, and blue are primary colors. Hues are made by mixing the primary colors. Secondary colors include orange, green, and violet. They are produced when equal amounts of primary colors are mixed together. For example, blue and yellow make green. Tertiary colors include red-orange, blue-green, red-violet, blue-violet, yellow-orange, and yellow-green. They are produced by mixing equal proportions of the primary colors and one of its secondary colors.

COLOR SCHEMES

A good color scheme is essential for designing beautiful jewelry. The color wheel can be used to develop harmony and unity in your design. Color schemes include mono-chromatic, analogous, complementary, split complementary, double complementary, and triad. A monochromatic scheme consists of one color or different values of one color. An example of a monochromatic color scheme is light green, green, and dark green, as seen in the *Envy* necklace.

Envy necklace by Marianne Filaggi

ANALOGOUS COLOR SCHEMES

An analogous color scheme uses colors near each other on the color wheel, such as red and red-orange.

Lampwork by Karen Leonardo, design by Sue Hart

COMPLEMEN-TARY COLOR SCHEMES

Complementary color schemes use colors directly across from each other on the color wheel, such as orange and blue.

Vivacious Beads by Karen Leonardo

DOUBLE COMPLEMENTARY COLORS

Double complementary colors have two colors and their complements. Triad colors contain three colors that lie an equal distance from each other around the color wheel, like blue, red, and yellow. Split complementary colors contain a main color and the two colors on either side of its complement. You can design jewelry using the color wheel and following specific color schemes, or you can bring out the hues in your lampworked beads.

COOL OR WARM COLORS

Colors can be categorized by cool or warm colors.

Cool colors have a base of green, blue, and violet, and tend to blend into the background.

Warm colors have a base of red, yellow, and orange and provide a more prominent look.

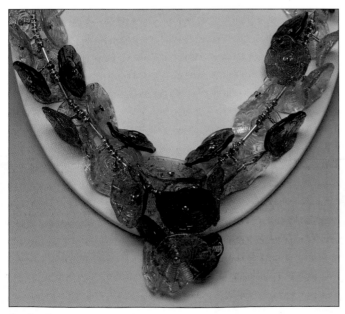

Cool color necklace by Marianne Filaggi

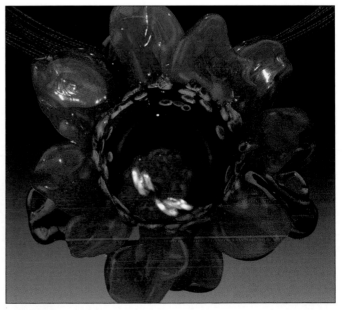

Warm color necklace by Debbie Weaver

TRENDS

Follow your instincts. If you aren't comfortable with choosing your color palette, you can look through magazines, study fashion and color trends, and observe clothing lines in stores. Clothing and jewelry lines tend to follow one another in color, so you will want to be aware of the current and future colors; you can find future colors at runway shows. Clothing lines, including holiday lines, tend to be in stores one season in advance so you can prepare your jewelry designs before the season.

Fall Clothing Line 7th St. Boutique, Indiana, PA

THE FOUR SEASONS

When designing jewelry, you may also want to follow the four seasons: spring, summer, fall, and winter. You will find that most people wear neutral or earthy colors with muted and warm tones in the fall, and most wear bright "sunny" tones in the summertime. Spring-time is perfect for pastels and the bright colors of Easter. The winter season calls out for reds, greens, and metallic gold and silver. Take these factors into account when designing your jewelry.

Necklace by Laurie Salopek

Jewelry-making Basics

Once you have your toolbox full of tools, bead-stringing materials, findings, and accent beads, you are ready to begin the projects in the book.

TOOLS

A toolbox is a great way to store your tools and various jewelry-making supplies. You can purchase a toolbox at your local hardware or craft store.

Almost all designers have a set of basic tools in their toolbox. Depending on the type of jewelry you are creating, there may be more tools required to finish your jewelry.

1. Roundnose pliers
2. Chainnose pliers
3. Hooknose pliers
4. Crimping pliers
5. Wire cutters
6. Scissors
7. Ruler
8. Hammer and block
9. Bead board
10. Glue
11. Beading needles and thread

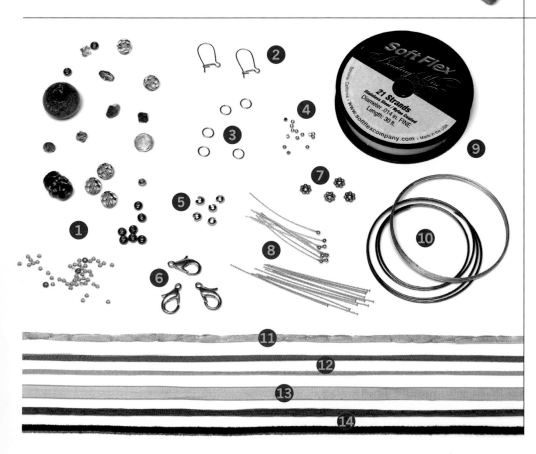

SUPPLIES

Basic supplies are what you need to complete a jewelry piece. These include:

1. Accent beads

Findings
2. Ear wires
3. Jump rings
4. Crimp beads
5. Crimp covers
6. Clasps
7. Spacers
8. Head Pins

Stringing materials
9. Flexible beading wire
10. Various types and sizes of metal wire
11. Silk
12. Suede cords
13. Ribbon
14. Leather

TECHNIQUES

Use these basic techniques in jewelry making to create the pieces you see on the following pages. You will learn how to crimp a crimp bead, attach a toggle or clasp, make loops, work with wire, and knot. As you practice and learn new techniques,

you will see how fun and exciting it is to make your own jewelry. Your friends will be asking you to make them something special, too. This is where the fun begins!

CLOSE CRIMP BEADS

Crimp beads hold a jewelry piece together neatly and securely. You can either fold a crimp bead with crimping pliers or flatten it with chainnose pliers. If you use a crimp cover to cover the crimp bead, fold the crimp instead of flattening it.

Flatten a crimp bead.

Fold a crimp bead with crimping pliers.

1 Crimp the crimp bead with your crimping pliers using the second groove from the tip of the pliers. It will flatten the crimp, capture the bead wire, and give it a groove. When you crimp the crimp bead again using the groove nearest the tip, it will fold in half neatly.

2 Crimp to fold in half.

3 Now you have a nice, neat crimp. If you wish, you can add a crimp cover to make it look even more professional.

ADD CRIMP COVERS

Adding a crimp cover finishes a jewelry piece and gives a professional look.

1 Put a cover over the crimp.

2 Gently pinch the cover closed with chainnose pliers.

USE FRENCH WIRE

You may choose to slide French wire (also called bullion) or Wire Guardians on your beading wire before adding your crimps to finish the jewelry piece. The clasp or toggle will fit directly over the French wire or Guardian. This material gives your jewelry a professional look and protects the wire.

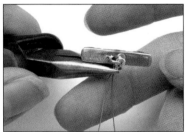

Wire guardian

ATTACH A TOGGLE OR CLASP

A toggle or clasp completes a jewelry piece and makes it wearable. There are two ways to attach a toggle with a crimp bead listed on the previous page. Be sure you have enough extra beading wire on the jewelry piece to complete this process. It is helpful to slide some of the beading wire back through a few of the beads.

1 String the end of the beading wire through the crimp, the toggle, and back through the crimp. String through a few beads and tighten the strand. Follow crimping directions.

2 Trim excess wire with wire cutters.

OPEN AND CLOSE A JUMP RING OR LOOP

Do not pull the jump rings from end-to-end, or you will distort the ring.

1 The proper way to open a jump ring or loop is to use two chainnose pliers, one in each hand. Grasp either side of the ring with the pliers so the gap is in the center.

2 Simultaneously move one hand away from you while moving the other hand toward you.

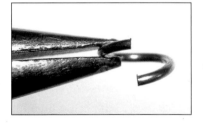

3 To close the jump ring, reverse the instructions: using two pliers, bring the ends toward the center.

WIRE WRAPPING A BRIOLETTE

Secure a briolette with wraps above the bead.

1 Center a briolette on a 2-in. (5cm) piece of wire, and bend both wire ends toward the top center of the bead.

2 Hold one wire straight with chain-nose pliers, and wrap the other wire around the first two or three times. Trim and tuck excess wire.

WRAPPED LOOPS

A wrapped loop allows you to close off the end of your wire or make a loop for an attachment.

1 Make sure you have at least 1¼ in. (3.2cm) of wire above the bead. Grasp the wire above the bead and make a right-angle bend.

2 Using roundnose pliers, position the jaws in the bend. Bring the wire over the top jaw of the roundnose pliers.

3 Reposition the pliers' lower jaw snugly into the loop. Curve the wire downward around the bottom of the roundnose pliers. This is the first half of a wrapped loop.

4 Grasp the wire end with chain-nose pliers, and wrap the wire end around itself to complete the wrap. Trim the excess wire. Tuck the cut wire end under the wrap for a smooth finish.

BASIC BEAD TECHNIQUES

LARK'S HEAD KNOT

Fold a cord in half and lay it behind a ring with the fold pointing down. Bring the ends through the ring from back to front, then through the fold and tighten.

OVERHAND KNOT

Make a loop and pull the short end of the thread through the loop and tighten.

SQUARE KNOT

Cross the left-hand thread over the right-hand thread, bring the thread under, and back up again.

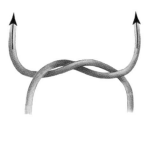

Next, cross the right-hand thread over the left-hand thread, go through the loop, and pull both thread ends at the same time to tighten.

SIMPLE LOOPS

Make simple loops to connect components or jump rings.

1 Trim the wire or head pin ⅜ in. (1cm) above the top bead. Make a right-angle bend close to the bead.

2 Grab the wire's tip with roundnose pliers. Roll the wire to form a half-circle. Release the wire.

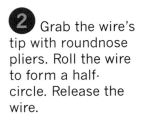

3 Reposition the pliers in the loop and continue rolling. The finished loop should form a centered circle above the bead.

TIPS

• When stringing a necklace with multiple strands, check the length of each strand. The strands should not overlap unless that's how you want the jewelry piece to look. The strand closest to the neck should be the shortest. A multiple-ring clasp is the best choice for a closure. When making a bracelet, strands should all be the same length.

• Wire is sold in various thicknesses, or gauges; the higher the gauge, the thinner the wire. 24-gauge wire is thin and flexible, while 18-gauge wire is thick and holds its shape well.

• Make a smooth bend in the wire by bending it over a ring mandrel or jig.

• Wire mars easily, so be careful when bending and hammering. Use emery paper to smooth out scratches.

• Always tuck in your cut ends so they don't catch on skin or clothing.

• You may want to make components that match for earrings.

• Stabilize beads with large bead holes by adding seed beads inside the holes.

SURGEON'S KNOT

A surgeon's knot is a square knot with an extra wrap through the first half of the knot. See Square Knot and add another wrap during the first step.

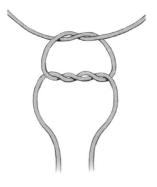

ADDING A THREAD

Sew into the project a few rows before the point where the last bead was added. Tie a few half-hitch knots between the beads and exit.

ENDING A THREAD

Weave the thread back into the beadwork, following the same thread path, and tie a few half-hitch knots between the beads. Switch directions as you weave so the thread crosses itself. Tie a few knots and trim excess thread.

STOP BEAD

A stop bead is used to temporarily secure beads when stitching your project. Be sure the bead is different from the beads used in the project. Add the bead at an end and sew through it twice for extra security.

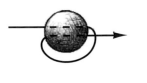

HALF-HITCH KNOT

Pass a needle under the thread between two bead. Cross over the thread between the beads, go through the loop, and pull.

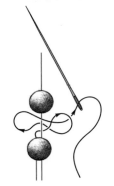

Spring is a wonderful season! A new year starts to bloom as hardy flowers begin to peek through the soil and the snow melts away. The grass turns green again, and signs of new life appear everywhere. Tiny crocuses start to show off their orange, white, and purple petals, while daffodils and tulips sway in the breeze. The birds are flittering around, chattering and singing. The trees begin to bud and show their full splendor, and woodland creatures wake up from a long winter's hibernation. It's definitely an occasion to celebrate with some brand-new jewelry.

Park your parka in the cedar chest, kick off your boots, and get ready to make some spring-inspired treasures. Browse through this collection of fresh colors and beautiful floral beads to see which projects call out to you.

Bead by Elise Strauss

Easter Parade
NECKLACE

SKILL LEVEL

Designed by Rickie Voges
Lampwork by Lezlie Belanger

Fresh, springtime beads combine beautifully with pearls and lampwork in delicate pastels. Use just a touch of silver, such as a clasp featuring a traditional Easter bloom. This design is simple but elegant and shows off charming figural artisan lampwork. These whimsical beads are all about bunnies, eggs, and the magic of spring!

1. Cut a piece of flexible beading wire to your desired necklace length, plus about 6 in. (15cm). String a crimp bead, ⅜-in. piece of French wire, and half of the clasp on one end of the beading wire. Go back through the crimp bead, and crimp (Basics).

2. String a daisy spacer, a rondelle, two bead caps back to back, six 10mm pearls, two bead caps back to back, a lampworked egg, a bead cap, a 6mm rice pearl, a bead cap, a lampworked egg, a bead cap, a lampworked bunny, a bead cap, and a lampworked egg. (As you string the beads on the wire, tuck the tail in as you go.)

String a bead cap, a 6mm rice pearl, a bead cap, a lampworked egg, two bead caps back to back, six 10 mm pearls, two bead caps back to back, six 10mm pearls, two bead caps, a lampworked egg, a bead cap, a 6mm rice pearl, a bead cap, and a lampworked egg.

String a bead cap, a 6mm rice pearl, a bead cap, a lampworked egg, two bead caps back to back, six 10mm pearls, two bead caps back to back, a rondelle, and a daisy spacer.

HELPFUL HINT

Finesse the strand a little by tugging and adjusting, until the strand is snug. When everything is in place, you are ready to close the final crimp. Clip as close to the last bead you threaded as possible with wire cutters. Don't cut the main beading wire strand, or you will have to re-string your necklace!

3. String a crimp bead, a ⅜-in. piece of French wire, and the remaining half of the clasp. Go back through the crimp bead and a few beads.

4. Check the fit and adjust if necessary. Pull the wire tight and crimp the crimp bead. Trim the excess beading wire.

THOUGHTS FROM THE DESIGNER —

I enjoy designing with unique lampworked beads because of the endless variety of styles available from individual artists. It's fun to combine handmade beads with gem-stones, precious metals, and out-of-the-ordinary findings to complement the original art bead. I always add just a special touch to surprise and delight.

Supplies
Finished size: 17 in. (43cm) without clasp
7 14mm lampworked egg-shaped beads
12 x 26mm lampworked bunny bead
2 4mm sterling daisy spacers
2 8mm crystal rondelles
24 6mm bead caps
24 10mm button pearls
4 6mm rice pearls
20mm decorative toggle clasp
Flexible beading wire, .019
2 sterling crimp beads
¾ in. (1.9cm) French wire

Tools
Chainnose pliers
Roundnose pliers
Wire cutters

Steel Magnolia
CHOKER

SKILL LEVEL

Fabulous flower beads need nothing more than a simple, bold chain for a stunning effect. This choker can be worn with the bead at the front or at the side. For a minimum amount of effort, you'll have a classy, stylish necklace that displays the unique bead to maximum advantage.

Designed by Sue Hart
Lampwork by Karen Leonardo

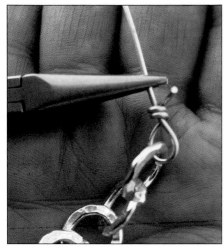

1. Cut a 6-in. (15cm) length of wire. String one wire end through an end link of chain. Make a wrapped loop (Basics).

2. String a 4mm silver bead and a lampworked flower bead onto the wire.

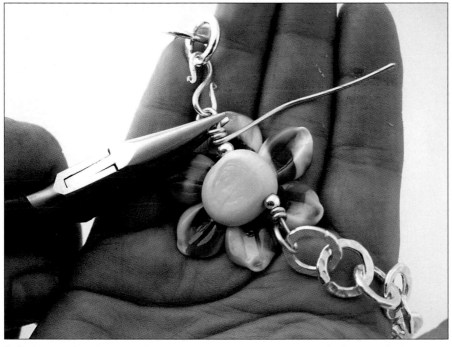

3. String another 4mm bead onto the wire, and snug it next to the lampworked bead's hole. Make a wrapped loop, and trim any excess wire. Place one end of the S-clasp hook into this loop, and squeeze gently closed. Hook the other end of the clasp into the end chain link to fasten the necklace.

HELPFUL HINT
If the chain links are not soldered, make sure they are closed firmly by gently pushing them with your pliers (see Basics).

THOUGHTS FROM THE DESIGNER—
Purchased chain makes this project easy for beginners, but if you want a challenge, you can design your own links. It's extremely satisfying to make something creative yourself. I get so many compliments when I wear this necklace!

Supplies
Finished size: 16 in. (41cm) choker
1⁵/₆ in. (4.1cm) lampworked flower bead
14 in. (36cm) 13mm link heavy hammered silver chain
6 in. (15cm) 16-gauge silver wire
17mm silver S-clasp
2 4mm silver beads

Tools
Roundnose pliers
Chainnose pliers
Wire cutters

Tulsa Spring Garden
SET

SKILL LEVEL ●●○

Tiny green leaves border purple blossoms in these lovely beads. Flower bead caps complement the spring theme, and sparkly crystals add a little bit of "bling." The dangles create interest and movement, and all the metal is sterling silver, which makes the jewelry durable and special. It is meant to last a lifetime.

Designed by Robin Bond, Lone Bird Designs
Lampwork by Judi Emerman

Earrings

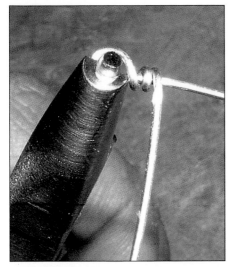

1. Cut a 5-in. (13cm) length of 22-gauge wire. About 2 in. (5cm) from the end of one wire, make a wrapped loop.

2. String a 6mm lilac crystal, a flower bead cap, a lampworked bead, and a bead cap. Make a wrapped loop above the bead cap.

3. Cut a 3-link and a 2-link piece of chain. Open a 6mm jump ring, and string an end link of both pieces of chain to make a dangle.

4. String the dangle from the bead cap end, and close the jump ring.

5. Use a 6mm jump ring to connect the other end of the dangle and an ear wire.

6. String a crystal on a head pin, and make a wrapped loop. Make three lilac dangles and two erinite.

7. Attach the dangles to your chains with 4mm jump rings. Start with the lilac dangle at the top of the 3-link and 2-link chain. Alternate colors on the chain. Repeat to make a second earring to match the first.

Bracelet

1. Cut five 6-in. (15cm) lengths of 22-gauge wire.

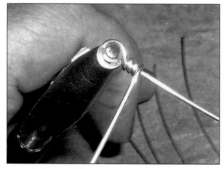

2. Approximately 2½ in. (6.4cm) from the end of a wire, make a wrapped loop.

3. String a 6mm crystal, a flower bead cap, a 10mm lampworked bead, a flower bead cap, and a crystal. Make a wrapped loop above the crystal.

4. Repeat steps 2 and 3 to create four more bracelet links, alternating crystal colors.

5. Open a 6mm jump ring, and connect a lilac and an erinite bracelet link.

6. Repeat with a second 6mm jump ring. You now have two jump rings securely holding the two links together.

7. Repeat steps 5 and 6 with other links until all links are joined, alternating the crystal color links.

8. Open a 6mm jump ring and connect a clasp half to an end link. Repeat on the other end.

9. String an erinite crystal, a flower bead cap, a lampworked bead, a flower bead cap, and erinite crystal on a head pin. Make a wrapped loop and attach the dangle to one end of the bracelet.

THOUGHTS FROM THE DESIGNER —

Most of the time, I don't have any idea what I'm going to design when I start the project. I sort the beads, place silver pieces, and try out crystals, gemstones, or Czech glass. I often feel like I'm throwing paint on a canvas and waiting to see what will happen. Once something sticks, I have a direction!

Supplies

Finished size: earrings, 2¾ in. (7cm), including ear wires
2 10mm round lampworked beads
8 6mm lilac crystals
4 flower bead caps
4 6mm erinite crystals
10 in. (25cm) 22-gauge wire
2 French ear wires
10 links 2mm chain
2 6mm jump rings
10 4mm jump rings
10 2-in. (5cm) head pins

bracelet, 8 in. (20cm) including toggle
6 10mm round lampworked beads
6 6mm lilac crystals
6 6mm erinite crystals
12 flower bead caps
Silver toggle clasp
30 in. (76cm) 22-gauge wire
10 6mm jump rings
2-in. (5cm) head pin

pendant, approx. 3 in. (7.6cm) long
16mm round lampworked bead
Silver pendant bail
7 in. (18cm) 22-gauge wire
5 6mm lilac crystals
3 6mm erinite crystals
6mm jump ring
7 4mm jump rings
2 flower bead caps
5 links 2mm chain
7 2-in. (5cm) head pins
10 seed beads (optional) for inside lampworked bead

Tools
Flatnose pliers
Roundnose pliers
Wire cutters

Pendant

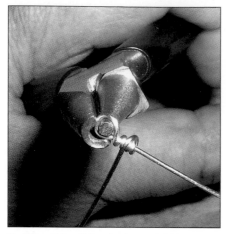

1. Cut a 7-in. (18cm) piece of 22-gauge wire. About 2½ in. (6.4cm) from one end of the wire, create a small wrapped loop (Basics).

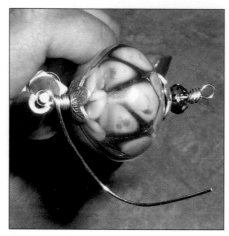

2. String a 6mm lilac crystal, a flower bead cap, a 16mm lampworked bead, and a flower bead cap. Make a wrapped loop, and trim the excess wire.

3. Open the back loop of the bail, and hang the pendant from the crystal end. Tighten the bail loop back snugly so the pendant hangs securely from the bail.

HELPFUL HINTS

When you are clipping the excess wire ends, they tend to shoot off erratically and could hit you in the face or in the eye. Safety glasses are recommended to prevent eye injuries.

Add tiny seed beads inside the lampworked beads to stabilize them and keep them from wobbling on the wire.

4. String a crystal on a head pin, and make a wrapped loop. Repeat to make a total of four lilac dangles and three erinite dangles.

5. Cut a 3-link and a 2-link length of chain. Open a 6mm jump ring (Basics), and string an end link of both pieces of chain. Attach to the end of the pendant.

6. Use 4mm jump rings to attach one crystal dangle to each link, alternating colors. Add a crystal dangle on each side, to the original 6mm jump ring.

Flower Chain Mail
NECKLACE

SKILL LEVEL

Designed by Lesley Jones
Lampwork by Kristan Child

The pasque flower, the inspiration for these beads, shows itself during early spring. It blooms on prairies and mountain slopes from Texas to Canada. Chain mail is elegant, classic, and requires only basic skills, but it will leave your fans in awe. This design is flexible and can work with almost any set of flat beads you may have. The goal is to create a sophisticated background for the dazzling lampwork.

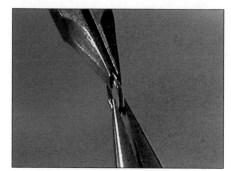

1. Close 12 6.5mm jump rings (Basics).

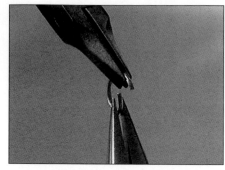

2. Open 24 6.5mm jump rings.

3. Use an open ring to pick up two closed rings. Gently close the open ring.

4. Use another open ring to go through the previous two closed rings and close it. This is called "doubling" the ring.

5. Use an open ring to go through all four closed rings: Close the ring.

HELPFUL HINT

Not all jump rings are created equal. With a nice, flush ring, you shouldn't even be able to tell that there is an opening. To get a perfect closed ring, choose precision-cut rings with flush ends. Generally, a supplier who specializes in chain mail will have precision-cut rings, and they will tumble-harden the rings for strength so you don't have to use solder. Usually a strong ring (preferably doubled) will do the trick on its own.

6. Repeat by putting another open ring through the same four closed rings and closing it. The six rings make a "rose" or "Celtic knot." (If the rings will not lie as pictured, flip over the two rings not lying properly. They lie flat when all the rings are flipped the same direction.)

7. Repeat steps 4–7 until you have made six roses.

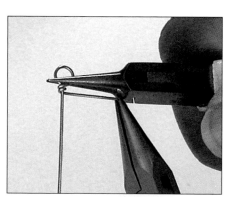

8. Cut a 4-in. (10cm) piece of wire and make a wrapped loop on one end. Wrap twice. Don't clip the long tail.

9. On the long wire tail, string a 3mm bicone crystal, a lampworked bead, and a 3mm crystal.

10. Make a wrapped loop (Basics) on the other end of the wire. Be sure to use the same spot on your pliers to make the loop the same size as the one in step 8.

THOUGHTS FROM THE DESIGNER—

What I love most about lampwork is the uniqueness of each piece. You can find just about any color combination in glass pieces. When working with lampworked beads, I always want to give them a setting that makes them the focus of the piece. The elegant look of the handwoven chain is a perfect high-class partner to the miniature glass works of art. It allows the lampworked pieces to still be the stars of the show!

Supplies
Finished size: 17–19 in. (43–48cm)
30 x 20mm lampworked pillow bead
4 20mm lampworked pillow beads
36 18-gauge 6.5mm jump rings
140 18-gauge 3.5mm jump rings
31 18-gauge 5mm jump rings
16-gauge 3mm jump ring
10 3mm bicone crystals
Clasp
6mm crystal
20 in. (51cm) 20– or 22–gauge
  half-hard wire
1 in. (2.5cm) head pin

Tools
Roundnose pliers
2 pairs of chainnose pliers
Wire cutters

11. Repeat steps 8–10 until all five lampworked beads are wrapped.

12. Open 64 3.5mm rings and close 64 3.5mm rings.

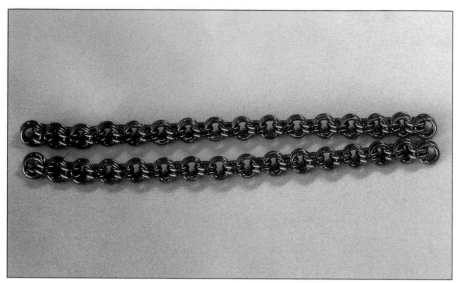

13. Using an open 3.5mm ring, pick up two closed rings and close the open ring. Double that ring, creating a two-in-two chain.

14. Continue until you have completed a 64-ring strand. Repeat steps 13 and 14 to make a second strand.

15. Open 24 5mm rings.

17. Use an open 5mm ring to go through the rose, and attach a 2mm lampworked bead unit. Close the ring and double the ring.

16. Use an open 5mm jump ring to go through the center of a rose and through the last two rings of a strand. Close this ring and double the ring.

19. Open a 3mm ring. Attach it to the clasp and one end of the necklace.

20. For a chain extension, open 12 3.5mm rings and close seven 5mm rings.

21. Using an open 3.5mm ring, attach a closed 5mm ring to the other end of the completed chain. Double the 3.5mm ring.

18. Repeat steps 16 and 17, using the open 5mm rings to attach the rest of the roses and lampworked bead units, placing the 20 x 20mm lampworked bead in the center.

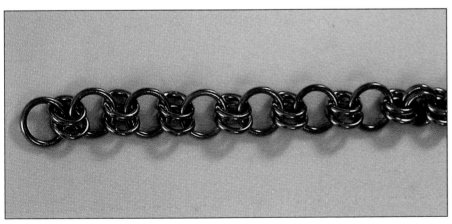

22. Repeat step 21 until all seven 5mm rings are attached.

23. String a 6mm crystal on a head pin. Make a wrapped loop and attach to the end jump ring before closing it.

Frog Eggs NECKLACE

SKILL LEVEL ●●●

Design and lampwork by Leslie Kaplan

The focal bead of this piece was created while exploring the vision of a lily pond necklace with borosilicate glass. The lily pad is covered with stacked dots in various colors of borosilicate glass, which gives the dots shimmering color. Despite the unromantic name, you will see glimmering reflections of the pond, the sky, and the water plants in the jelly-like "frog eggs" on top of the lily pad. The large, dramatic bead is paired with a robust spiral peyote rope, which complements the color, size, and design of the bead.

1. Cut a piece of Fireline 1½ times as long as your arm. Thread a needle on one end.

HELPFUL HINT

When using Fireline, flatten the end of the line with chainnose pliers to help thread the needle.

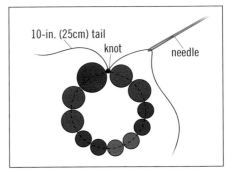

2. Rows 1 and 2: String on the Fireline in this order: one 6º bead, two 8º, two 11º (color 1), two 11º (color 2), two 11º (color 1), and two 8º beads. Push the beads down to about 10 in. (25cm) from the end of the thread, and tie the beads into a ring with a double knot.

This will form the first and second row of beads. The third row is the hardest, but it sets the pattern for the rest of the tube. Pull tight after each stitch, and encourage the tube shape to form. The color and size bead that your needle is exiting should always be the color and size of the next bead you are placing. Stitch through every other bead.

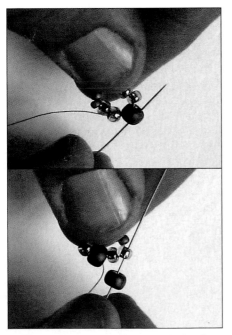

3. Row 3: Put the needle through the 6º, pick up a 6º on your needle and stitch through the second 8º bead, so that the new 6º lies on top of the first (or next) 8º.

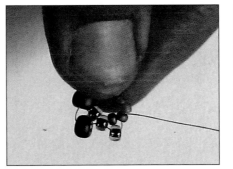

Pull tight. Pick up an 8º on the needle and stitch through the second 11º bead (color 1), so that the 8º lies on top of the first 11º bead (color 1).

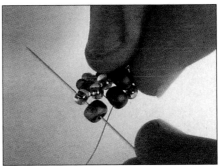

Pull tight. Pick up an 11º bead (color 1) on the needle and stitch through the second 11º bead (color 2), so that the 11º lies on top of the first 11º (color 2) bead. Pick up an 11º bead (color 2) on the needle and stitch through the second 11º bead (color 1), so that the 11º (color 2) lies on top of the first 11º (color 1) bead. Pick up a third 11º bead (color 1) and stitch through the second 8º that is next, so that the 11º (color 1) lies on top of the first 8º bead. Pick up an 8º bead and stitch through the second 6º that is next, so that the 8º lies on top of the first 6º bead. To begin the next row, pick up a 6º bead and stitch through the second 8º.

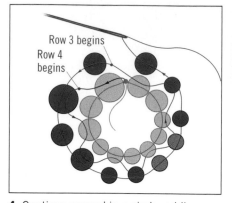

4. Continue around in a circle, adding beads in the same pattern. Each bead that you pick up should be the same kind and size as the bead that your needle just exited, creating a spiral effect. After the first row, every other bead on the "working edge" will be higher than the others. You will effectively be filling in the "bricks on the wall" each time you take a stitch, with the new bead filling in the empty space and your needle going through the next raised bead. The different-sized beads will make your tube undulate interestingly.

5. Stop stitching when your Fireline is about 5 in. (13cm) long, and your needle is exiting an 11º. Measure out another comfortable length of Fireline and thread a second needle. Slip the second needle into an 11º bead a few rows back, and run the new needle and thread through a couple of the adjacent beads. Sew under an existing thread between two beads and tie a half-hitch knot around it with your new thread. Run the new thread through a few more beads until it exits the same 8º bead in the same direction as needle #1. Tie the two threads together in a square knot. Use the first needle to run the short end back through the bead it is coming out of and back and forth through a few adjacent beads. Cut off the remaining Fireline so the free end does not show. Continue the pattern with the new needle and thread.

6. Continue adding beads in this pattern until the tube equals half the desired length of the necklace, minus the clasp and the focal bead. End with the needle coming out of a 6º bead. (This will be one side of the necklace, from the clasp to the focal.) Even out one end of the spiral rope so that it will fit snugly against the focal bead: Pick up an 8º on the needle instead of a 6º. Stitch through the next 8, then add beads in the regular pattern until the needle is exiting the last 11º in the row. Stitch through the next 8º, 6º, and the next 8º without adding beads. Add an 8º and continue the patterns adding three 11º beads. Run the needle through all the beads to secure the end and leave a 10-in. (25cm) tail.

Repeat steps 1–6 to make the other side of the peyote spiral rope.

7. Cut a piece of 22-gauge wire 4 in. (10cm) longer than the length of both tubes and the focal bead added together (in this case, 21 in./53cm). Beginning at the uneven edge, carefully thread the wire through one peyote tube, then through the focal bead and then through the evened-off edge of the second tube and out the end. Add needles to the free ends of the Fireline at each end of the focal bead. (The needles need to be long enough to reach through the bead.) Leave some working room between the ends of the peyote spiral and the focal bead; stitch through the bead from each end.

On each side of the focal, stitch through the 6º bead, and then back through the focal bead to the other side. Stitch through one of the 11º beads on each side and pass the needles back through the focal bead. Stitch through an 8º on each side, and back through the focal one last time. Snug the tubes up to the focal bead by pulling gently on both needles at the same time to take the slack out of the stitches.

Secure the Fireline on both sides by burying the end in the spiral: Run the needle through several beads, making a half-hitch knot around an earlier stitch, and running the needle through several more beads, preferably 11ºs. Clip thread closely.

HELPFUL HINT

To customize your peyote spiral, try replacing the 6º with a drop or cube bead or even a small glass pearl. 11º triangles nest together for a neat flat finish if you use at least two rows of them. It's nice to alternate matte finish and shiny beads to maximize contrast and zip!

8. Finish the tubes: Thread a needle onto the free end of a tube. Reduce the end of the spiral rope so it fits fairly snugly around the wire. Thread should be exiting the 6º. Stitch through the second 8º without adding a bead. Pull snug. Add an 11º (color 1) and stitch through the next high 11º. Stitch through the next high 11º (color 2) without adding a bead. Pull snug. Pick up an 11º (color 2) and stitch through the next high 11º (color 1). Stitch through the next 8º, 6º, 8º, and 11º without adding beads. Pick up an 11º (color 1) and stitch through the next high 11º (color 2). Stitch through the next 8º and 6º without adding beads. String one 6º and then one 8º bead over the end of the silver wire and stitch the needle through both beads. Bring the needle back through the 6º and bury the end in the beads of the peyote spiral, in a similar way to the end of step 7.

9. Using the chainnose pliers, bend the silver wire at a 90-degree angle (right angle) about 3mm from the end of the peyote spiral. Using roundnose pliers, make a loop in the wire big enough for the clasp loop to fit.

2 in. (5cm) of silver wire will be exposed. Repeat step 8 for the other side.

10. Slip one side of the clasp onto the wire loop.

11. Holding the loop securely with the chainnose pliers, wrap the free end of the wire around the wire stem several times. Clip off closely.

Repeat on the other side of the necklace with the other half of the clasp, making sure everything is snug.

THOUGHTS FROM THE DESIGNER —

I love using spiral peyote. It gives me great flexibility with design and color because there is an infinite combination of sizes, finishes, and shapes of seed beads. I love pulling out the color of lampworked beads by stringing them with complementary seed beads and semiprecious stones. Seed beads come in such luscious colors and finishes—I am particularly fond of matte Aurora Borealis (AB) finishes. I aim for a subtle but bold effect, making sure the lamp-worked bead is highlighted but not overpowered.

Supplies
Finished size: 17 in. (43cm)
40mm lampworked focal bead
1½ large tubes of Myuki 6º seed beads, matte black AB
1 large tube Myuki 8º seed beads, black color-lined multi AB
½ large tube 11º, opaque matte amethyst purple (color 1)
½ large tube Toho 11º seed beads, gold matte AB (color 2)
Fireline, 6 lb. test, about 10 yd.
20–22 in. silver wire, 22-gauge

Tools
2 beading needles, size 12
Chainnose pliers
Wire cutters

"Think Green" Silver Clay
CORE BEAD

Did you ever have a nice large-hole bead that you wanted to wear as a pendant, but you didn't like the unfinished core? Here is your answer. Line the bead with metal clay paste in less than an hour. You can add the bead to a chain, ribbons, leather, or a premade silk necklace. It's easy, fun, and ready to wear with any outfit!

SKILL LEVEL

Designed by Shruti Gautam Dev
Lampwork by Nicole Valentine-Rimmer

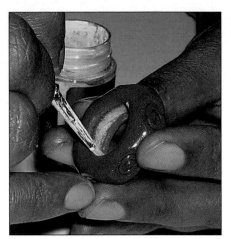

1. Clean the bead and core with an alcohol wipe.

2. Apply a thick layer of silver clay paste to the core with a paintbrush. Let dry. Repeat.

3. Wipe the rim of the bead clean on both sides to remove any unwanted silver paste. Let dry.

4. Put the bead on a fiber sheet or blanket in a core kiln, and ramp up the temperature gradually. Fire at 1200°F (650°C) for 30 minutes. Let the kiln cool.

5. Brush off the fire scale with a steel brush and string the bead on a ribbon or chain.

HELPFUL HINTS

Work with clean hands, and wipe the bead clean (except where the paste has been applied) before firing.

Do not fire the bead at more than 1200°F. A hotter temperature might distort the shape of the glass bead.

THOUGHTS FROM THE DESIGNER—

I find it fascinating to be able to fuse glass and silver so effortlessly for such a stunning result. Adding a silver core to a lampworked bead gives an unexpected dimension to the bead. A quiet, elegant glass bead is dressed up just that wee bit and ready to party!

Supplies
Glass beads with big cores
Silver clay paste
Ribbon or purchased chain

Tools
Soft paintbrush
Wet wipes (alcohol based)
Kiln
Fiber sheet or blanket
Steel brush

Summer is the time for relaxing, taking a break, and just having fun! Vacation plans are on our minds: where should we go, what do we want to see, how far should we travel? Should we hike through the mountains, tan at the beach, or take a cruise? There is so much to do, but so little time—or at least, that's how it seems!

Take a few hours to create summer jewelry designs. This oh-so-hot collection has plenty of pieces that are perfect for steamy summer days and nights!

Bead by Elise Strauss

Under the Sea
BRACELET

Sun, fun, and summer fantasies liven up this bracelet. Let your imagination run wild as you think of sand, a cool beverage, and your new jewelry. The design is so easy, you can make it in minutes.

SKILL
LEVEL

Lampwork and design by Amy Cornett

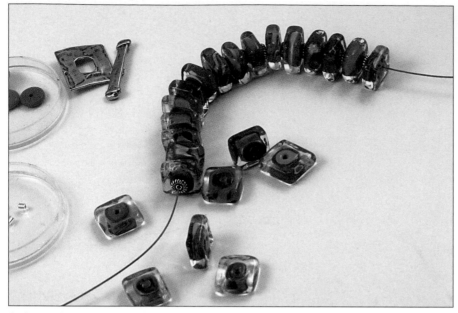

1. Cut a 10-in. (25cm) strand of beading wire. Alternate spacers and disc beads until all of the lampworked discs are strung.

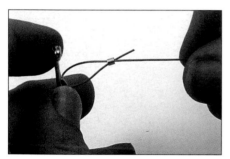

2. String two crimp beads and half a clasp on one end. Loop the wire back through the crimp beads, and make a folded crimp on each (Basics).

3. On the other end, string a 9mm round, a 7mm disc, a 9mm round, a 7mm disc, and a 5mm spacer.

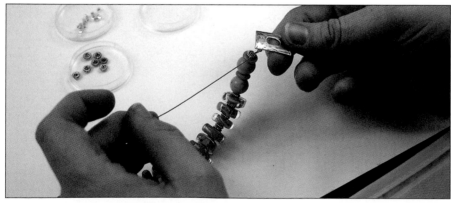

4. Tighten the strand, and adjust the fit if necessary. Repeat step 2, substituting the remaining clasp half. Trim any excess wire.

HELPFUL HINT

You can add more silver disc beads or lampworked beads to make a longer bracelet.

THOUGHTS FROM THE DESIGNER —

Could the sea be our most prolific source of inspiration? Like so many artisans, I, too, am drawn to the shore. For a Midwestern girl like myself, the sea is very far away. Since my tootsies are relegated to dry land for the meantime, my aquatic fantasies take life in this bracelet made of glass, turquoise, and silver. I can live with that!

Supplies
Finished size: 7 in. (18cm) without clasp
22–24 square lampworked disc beads
2 9mm turquoise rounds
2 7mm green turquoise discs
27–30 5mm Bali silver spacers
Silver toggle clasp
4 crimp beads
Flexible beading wire, .018 or .019

Tools
Wire cutters
Crimping pliers

Do You Know the Way to San José?

SKILL LEVEL ●●○

NECKLACE

Designed by Vicki Wegener of Victoria Perkins Studio
Lampwork by Darlene Durrwachter-Rushing

This lampworked bead set presented unique opportunities and challenges. The blue and white beads are lovely, original, and full of color. Old, orange Nga beads from the northeast corner of India add extra pop, and silver foil-wrapped beads give the necklace sparkle and textural complexity. Finally, the clasp pulls the other elements of the piece together.

HELPFUL HINT

Use a design board. It keeps the beads from rolling around, and it has a marked ruler to keep track of the length of the piece. You can also use a measuring tape and a piece of suede or a cotton kitchen towel in a neutral shade.

1. Using a design board, lay the beads out the way they will be strung. Place the 26mm focal in the center of the board. On each side, place a 12mm spacer, an 8mm silver, a Nga, a 12mm spacer, a 10mm round, a 12mm spacer, a 14mm foil, and a 22mm oval.

On each side, place a 15mm silver, a 22mm round, a Nga, a 12mm spacer, a 10mm spacer, a 12mm spacer, an 8mm silver, a 22mm oval, and a 14mm foil. Place a spiral spacer between each bead and on each end.

2. Cut 27 in. (69cm) of beading wire. Transfer the beads from the bead board to the beading wire, following the design as you string. When you are finished stringing, tape the ends and hold the piece up to make sure that it looks good and hangs well as a finished piece. Adjust if necessary.

3. String a crimp bead and half of the clasp. Go back through the crimp bead, string the wire through the next couple of beads, and tighten until the strand is snug. Crimp the crimp bead (Basics). Repeat to add the second clasp half. Close a crimp cover over each crimp bead. Trim the excess beading wire.

THOUGHTS FROM THE DESIGNER—

Jewelry is part of a tradition of adornment dating back to at least 38,000 BC. I keep that in mind while stringing beads and adding stones, crystals, metals, pearls, and wood. Each piece will have its own journey from the torch of a lampworker to the person who ultimately wears the jewelry. It is always exciting to settle down in the studio and create jewelry using lampworked beads.

Supplies
Finished size: 21 in. (53cm) without clasp
10 12mm turquoise lampworked
 spacers
4 10mm ivory and turquoise lampworked rounds
2 22mm ivory and turquoise lampworked rounds
26mm ivory and turquoise lampworked
 focal round
4 15 x 22mm turquoise oval beads
4 14mm silver foil-wrapped beads
4 orange Nga beads
2 15mm Bali silver beads
4 8mm Bali silver beads
36 Thai silver spiral spacers
Silver toggle clasp with chain
2 crimp beads
2 crimp covers
Flexible beading wire, .018 or .019

Tools
Wire cutter
Crimping pliers
Design board

Incan Queen
BRACELET

This lovely bracelet resembles an ancient treasure fit for a queen. Rich gold and subtle silver flecks give a royal look, and intricate Bali silver beads mimic the scrolled details of these stunning lampworked beads. Use flat, squeezed beads that allow the bracelet to lie comfortably against the wrist.

SKILL
LEVEL

Designed by Rickie Voges
Lampwork by Sue Booth

1. String a 3mm round on a 1-in. (2.5cm) eye pin; repeat twice. String a 4mm spacer, a 6mm lampworked spacer, and a 4mm spacer on a 1-in. (2.5cm) eye pin; repeat twice. String a 6mm bead cap, a 10mm Bali bead, and a 6mm bead cap on a 2-in. (5cm) eye pin. Make the first half of a wrapped loop (Basics) above all the beads.

2. Connect a 6mm lampworked spacer component to one end of the chain, and complete the wraps. Repeat near the other end of the chain, skipping the last few links.

3. Divide the chain into ¾-in. (1.9cm) and 1¼-in. (3.2cm) sections. Connect the Bali bead component through the soldered jump ring and the middle chain link, and complete the wraps. (The chain should be between the wraps and the Bali component.)

HELPFUL HINT

Bracelets tend to slide around your wrist no matter how carefully you balance pieces. Choosing a stylish toggle adds to the design and gives your bracelet a polished, professional look.

THOUGHTS FROM THE DESIGNER —

I began this project by pulling together gold vermeil, silver, and gemstones to see which materials balanced nicely with the lampworked beads. I chose to use garnets and Bali silver to enhance the main focus of my design: beautiful, hand-made artisan beads.

Supplies
Finished size: 6½ in. (16.5cm) without the clasp
4 18mm artisan lampworked beads
2 3mm artisan lampworked bead
3 6mm lampworked spacer beads
4 10–12mm sterling Bali beads (2 barrels, 2 rounds)
10mm sterling Bali bead for charm
6 4mm garnet round beads
4 3mm faceted garnet beads
8 6mm vermeil bead caps
11 4mm vermeil daisy spacers
6mm soldered jump ring
7 1-in (2.5cm) 26-gauge eye pins
2-in. (5cm) 22-gauge eye pin
2-in. (5cm) fine-link (2mm) chain
14 in. (36cm) 19-strand beading wire
¾ in. (1.9cm) French wire
2 sterling crimp beads
20–22mm toggle clasp

Tools
Chainnose pliers
Roundnose pliers
Wire cutters

HELPFUL HINT
Use French wire to cover the beading wire and give your jewelry a professional look. Be sure the French wire ends are flush against the crimp bead, covering the beading wire that loops through the post end of your toggle.

4. Connect a lampworked component to the closed jump ring, and connect the rest of the charms to the chain wherever you like. Complete the wraps, and set the charm dangle aside.

5. String a crimp bead, a ⅜-in. (1cm) piece of French wire, and the bar end of the toggle clasp on a 14-in. (36cm) piece of beading wire. Pass the beading wire back through the crimp bead, leaving a 3-in. (7.6cm) tail, and pull tight. Crimp (Basics).

6. String two 4mm spacers, an 18mm lampworked bead, a 4mm spacer, a 10mm round, a bead cap, a 4mm round, an 18mm, a 4mm round, a bead cap, a 12mm barrel, a bead cap, a 4mm round, and a 23mm. Repeat in reverse order, beginning with a 4mm round and ending with just one 4mm spacer. Add the charm dangle from step 4.

7. Slide on a crimp bead, French wire, and the loop end of the clasp.

8. Pass the beading wire back through the crimp bead. Thread the wire through about 2 in. (5cm) of the strung bracelet and through the second lampworked bead from the end. Tug slightly, and adjust until the strand is snug with no excess slack. Check and adjust the fit if necessary. Crimp the crimp bead and trim the excess wire.

Chunky Cheer
BRACELET

This chunky bracelet has the sophisticated look of black and silver with an added dash of color from the cheery lampworked beads. Matte black onyx offers a nice contrast to the shiny glass. This bracelet is simple and easy to complete in just half an hour—why not take the time to create a great piece of jewelry?

SKILL LEVEL

Designed by Lisa Liddy, Joolz by Lisa
Lampwork by Marilyn Martin

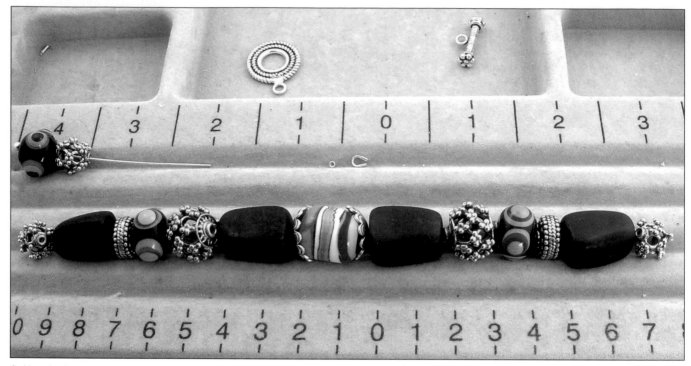

1. Use the bead board to lay out your design. Lay out a 10mm Bali filigree bead, an onyx bead, a Bali rondelle, a lampworked bead, a 12 x 18mm Bali filigree bead, an onyx bead, a bead cap, and a lampworked bead. Reverse order to finish the bracelet.

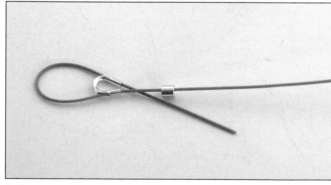

2. Cut 12 in. (30cm) of beading wire, and thread one end through a crimp bead and through the ends of the Wire Guardian as shown. Add half of the clasp, and thread the short end of the beading wire through the crimp bead. Crimp the crimp bead (Basics) and trim any excess wire.

3. String the bracelet. When you have strung all of the beads, use a BeadStopper to keep the beads in place as you test the size of the bracelet on your wrist.

HELPFUL HINT

The springy BeadStopper eliminates stringing mishaps before you finish the ends. No more, "Oops, the beads just spilled everywhere!"

4. If necessary, add smaller silver spacers to lengthen the bracelet and give flexibility to the clasp. Repeat step 2 to finish the bracelet, substituting the remaining clasp half.

5. String a spacer, a glass lampworked bead, and a silver bead on a head pin. Make the first half of a wrapped loop (Basics), attach the dangle onto the ring of the loop end of the toggle, and complete the wraps.

THOUGHTS FROM THE DESIGNER —

This piece rolled around in my head for awhile until I came up with a design that worked. I kept thinking I needed more lampworked beads, but I only had four of them to use. So playing off the colors and variations in the lampworked beads, I added some different kinds of silver beads and used chunks of onyx to tie all of the pieces together.

Supplies
Finished size: 7¾ in. (19.7cm) without clasp
4 lampworked beads, round or barrel-shaped (size can vary)
4 10 x 20mm matte onyx nugget-style beads
2 15mm Hill Tribe silver bead caps
2 12 x 18mm Bali silver beads
3 10mm Bali silver filigree beads
2 5 x 15mm Bali silver rondelles
2–5 2mm silver spacers (optional)
Toggle clasp
2 in. (5cm) silver head pin
2 Wire Guardians
2 2mm crimp beads
Flexible beading wire, .012 or .013

Tools
Roundnose pliers
Crimping pliers
Wire cutters
Design board
BeadStopper (optional)

Sweet Treats Charm
BRACELET
& EARRINGS

SKILL
LEVEL

Designed by Lisa Liddy, Joolz by Lisa
Lampwork by Lezlie Belanger

What lady doesn't like her sweets? They're oh-so-yummy, but with too many calories, you've gotta watch those hips and thighs. Luckily, you can wear these guilt-free treats on your wrists all day long. The tiny glass confections look good enough to eat—how can you resist the temptation? Mmmm!

Bracelet

1. Lay out all the components and assemble the dangles using head pins and daisy spacers (as desired). Make six or seven 8mm rose crystal dangles; five or six 8mm rose alabaster crystal dangles; five 13mm coin pearl dangles; and eight or nine daisy spacer and lampworked-bead dangles.

Reserve one lampworked dangle for a decorative dangle on the end of the bracelet.

2. Thread a 5-in. (13cm) piece of beading wire through a crimp bead and a Wire Guardian. Thread the end chain link through the Wire Guardian loop, and go back through the crimp bead. Snug the wire, and crimp the crimp bead (Basics). Repeat on the other end of the chain. Trim any excess wire, leaving about a 1-in. (2.5cm) tail.

HELPFUL HINT

I used a variety of head pins in this project because of the different-sized holes in the pearls, crystals, and lampworked beads. You may want to purchase a few extra head pins to be sure you have enough. If the bead's hole is too big, string a spacer first to hold it in place.

THOUGHTS FROM THE DESIGNER —

These beads seemed to say "charm bracelet," but I didn't want them to disappear from view around the wrist. I decided to incorporate Hill Tribe silver tube bangles and cluster the charms, crystals, and pearls toward the center of the bracelet for more visual impact.

Supplies
Finished size: bracelet, 7½ in. (19.1cm) without clasp
8–9 lampworked beads, ice cream cones and cakes
5 13mm white coin pearls
4 12mm Hill Tribe silver hammered discs
6–7 8mm crystal balls in rose
5–6 8mm crystal balls in rose alabaster
2 Hill Tribe silver curved tubes (45mm)
13mm silver square toggle clasp
3 in. (7.6cm) Halstead chain with 10mm links
4 Wire Guardians
4 crimp beads
20–22 3–4mm daisy spacers
30–35 18–20-gauge decorative head pins
5 22–24-gauge decorative head pins
Flexible beading wire, .018 or .019

Earrings
2 lampworked cake beads
2 8mm crystal balls in rose
6 3–4mm daisy spacers
2 6mm round beads
2 ear wires
2 18–20-gauge decorative head pins
2 20–22-gauge eye pins

Tools
Roundnose pliers
Chainnose pliers
Crimping pliers
Wire cutters
Bead board

HELPFUL HINT

The Wire Guardian helps protect the stringing wire from wear and tear, which prolongs the life of your jewelry piece.

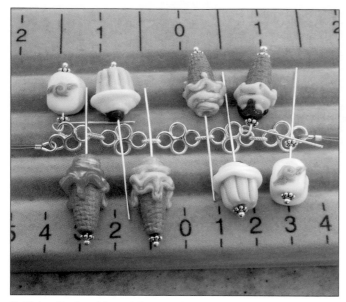

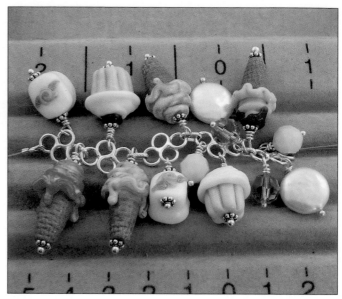

3. Using the bead board, lay out the chain base, and place lampworked bead dangles on the chain to determine the order and pattern. Take into account the size and colors of the lamp-worked beads, as well as the textures and colors of the other crystals and pearls.

4. Attach the lampworked bead dangles, pearl dangles, and crystal dangles using wrapped loops (Basics). Fill in where there are holes until you are satisfied with the look.

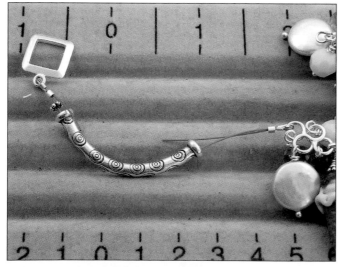

5. Slide one of the Hill Tribe silver tubes on the wire, tucking the tail ends into the tube. String a daisy spacer, a crimp bead, a Wire Guardian, and half of the clasp. Go back through the Wire Guardian and crimp bead. Snug the beads on the wire, and crimp the crimp bead. Repeat on the other end of the bracelet, substituting the remaining clasp half.

6. On a head pin, string a daisy spacer, the lampworked bead reserved for the dangle, and another daisy spacer. Attach the head pin to the loop end of the toggle with a wrapped loop. Trim the excess wire.

Earrings

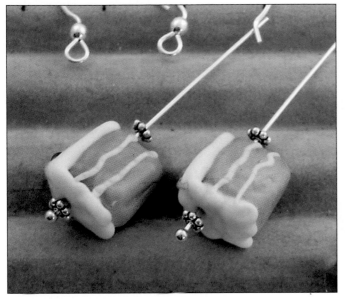

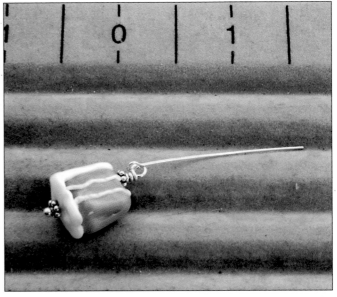

1. String a daisy spacer, a lampworked bead, and a daisy spacer on a head pin. Repeat.

2. Make the first half of a wrapped loop above the lampworked bead. String the loop of an eye pin, and finish the wraps.

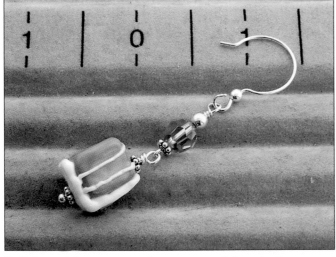

3. String a daisy spacer, an 8mm rose crystal, and a 6mm round on the eye pin. Make a wrapped loop to attach the eye pin to an ear wire. Repeat steps 2 and 3 to finish the other earring.

Designed by Cary Martin
Lampwork by Lezlie Belanger

The colors in this necklace exude tranquil serenity reminiscent of a stroll on a sandy beach. Softly etched lampworked beads evoke ocean-worn sea glass, along with natural matte Karen Hill Tribe and Thai silver. The jewelry design sets the stage for a relaxing time sipping your piña colada under an umbrella on some remote island.

S Links

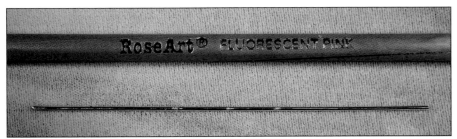

1. Cut eight 4-in. (10cm) sections of 18-gauge wire. With a colored pencil, mark the center of each piece of wire (at 2 in./5cm). Measure outward from the center ½ in. (1.3cm) on each side and mark this as well.

2. Place the edge of your colored pencil on the inside of the ½-in. (1.3cm) measurement to the right of center.

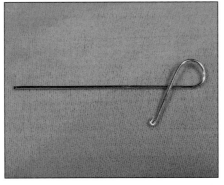

3. Bend the wire away from you around the pencil and back toward you, ending with the tail over the center mark. Bend the tip of the wire around on itself slightly.

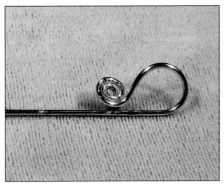

4. Using chainnose pliers, spiral the wire tip up until it just crosses the center mark.

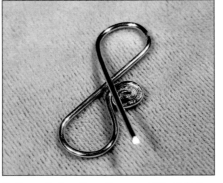

5. Repeat step 3 on the opposite end of the wire, bending the wire in the opposite direction.

Teahouse
NECKLACE

Warm brown, taupe, and pumpkin beads are perfect for the autumn season. Imagine sitting in your home relaxing, sipping tea, and enjoying the cool nights and whispering of the leaves outside. Your evenings are getting longer, and you have more time to design jewelry. Why not try this one?

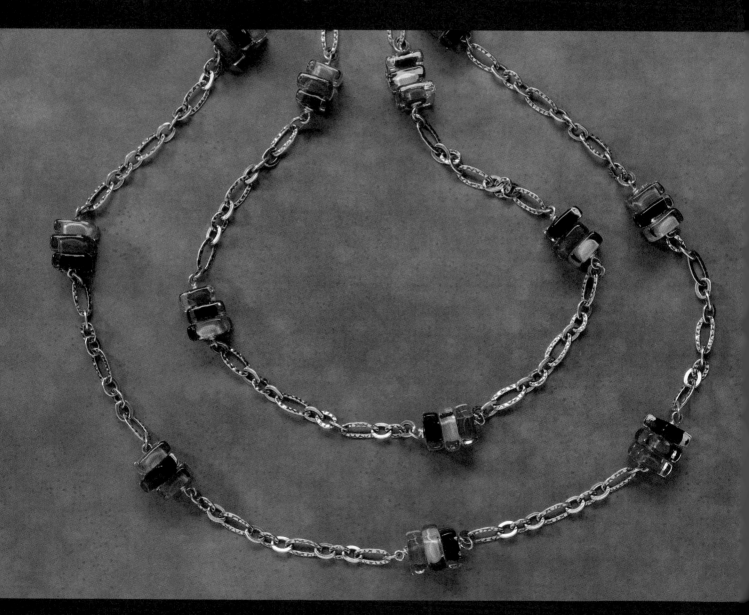

Design and lampwork by Amy Cornett

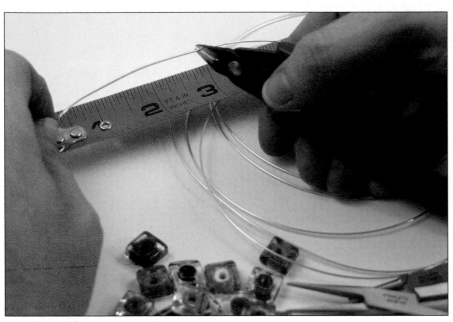

1. Cut the wire into 12 3-in. (7.6cm) lengths. Cut the chain into 12 3-in. (7.6cm) lengths.

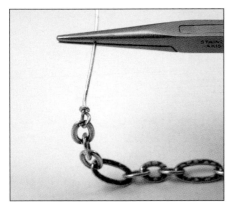

2. Make the first half of a wrapped loop on one wire (Basics). Attach to one end of the chain. Finish wrapping the loop.

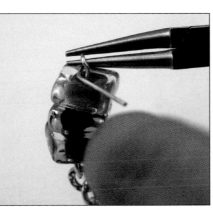

3. String three lampworked beads and make the first half of a wrapped loop above the beads.

4. Attach a length of chain and complete the wraps.

5. Repeat steps 2–4 to finish the necklace. Attach the last lampworked link to the end of the first length of chain.

THOUGHTS FROM THE DESIGNER—

Everyday living is my greatest source of inspiration for the beads and jewelry I create; I often discover the most inventive color combinations and textures in my surroundings. The packaging for my favorite tea blend was the jumping off point for the Teahouse Necklace. Its sophisticated shape and color palette worked seamlessly into this simple, elegant piece.

Supplies
Finished size: 42 in. (1.06m)
36 lampworked square stack beads
36 in. (.9m) hammered oxidized link chain
36 in. (.9m) 20-gauge silver half-hard wire

Tools
Roundnose pliers
Chainnose pliers
Wire cutters

Fall Ribbons
NECKLACE

The fabulous muted colors of silk ribbons mixed with sparkling lampworked beads are a reminder of wonderful autumn days when the sun comes up and burns away the mist.

SKILL LEVEL ●●○

Designed by Sue Hart
Lampwork by Kristan Child

1. Pass the thread on one end of a silk ribbon through the loop on a charm and make an overhand knot (Basics). Repeat several times until the charm is secure, and then cut off excess thread. Put a small dab of glue on the cut end of the thread to prevent raveling. Repeat with remaining ribbons and charms.

HELPFUL HINT

The ribbons for this necklace are quite delicate; handle them carefully. Iron the ribbons once the necklace is finished, so they look crisp. Stagger the ends of the ribbons to create a cascade down the front of the necklace.

THOUGHTS FROM THE DESIGNER —

I love the challenge of working with a variety of materials and finding ways of combining different textures and colors. The fluidity of the silk ribbons mixed with the semiprecious stones and special lampworked beads make this necklace extremely tactile. It's also very comfortable to wear.

2. On a rolled ribbon end, thread a lampworked disc bead and slide it 12 in. (30cm) along. Tie an overhand knot in the ribbon next to the bead. Thread a 5mm jump ring onto the ribbon, and tie a knot around the ring 4 in. (10cm) from the end of the ribbon. Thread a bead and a jump ring, and tie a knot 2 in. (5cm) along the ribbon. Thread a bead and a jump ring, and tie a knot at the end of the ribbon. Trim any excess ribbon, and dab the end with glue to prevent raveling. Repeat with the remaining ribbon.

Repeat at the other end of each ribbon, but this time secure the first bead 9 in. (23cm) from the end of the ribbon.

Supplies
Finished size: 24 in. (61cm)
10–15 12mm disc lampworked beads
3 39-in. (.99m) silk ribbons, 12mm wide*
2 39-in. (.99m) rolled silk ribbons, 3mm wide
6 assorted 12mm silver charms
12 10–12mm semiprecious beads, 4 of each color
12 2-in. (5cm) 22-gauge silver head pins
24 2mm silver round beads
10 in. (25cm) 22-gauge wire
12 5mm closed silver jump rings
Instant glue or fabric glue
8 in. (20cm) strand coordinating small chip beads
*Please note: The wider ribbons used have threads attached at either end for attaching charms. If yours don't have attached threads, sew matching colored threads on the ribbons.

Tools
Roundnose pliers
Chainnose pliers
Wire cutters

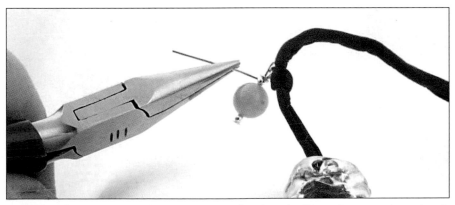

3. String a 2mm silver round, a semiprecious bead, and a 2mm silver round on a head pin, and make the first half of a wrapped loop (Basics). Attach a jump ring (Basics) and complete the wraps. Coordinate the beads to the colors of the ribbons, and put one of each color onto its corresponding ribbon end.

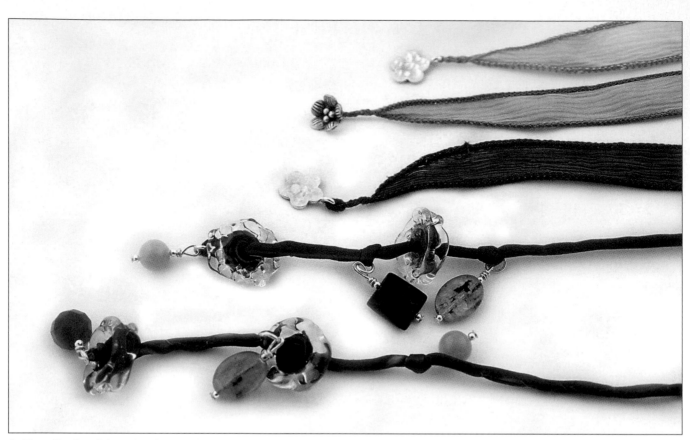

4. Place the five ribbons in a line, and stagger the ends by about 1 in. (2.5cm). This will ensure that when you form the loop, the ends of the ribbons will fall at different lengths.

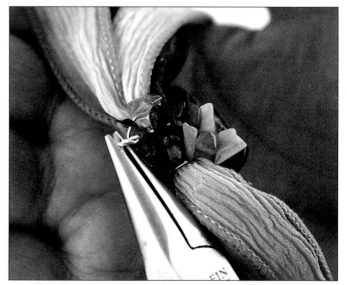

5. Fold the ribbons in half, making sure that the wide ribbons are flat. About 13 in. (33cm) from the center fold, wrap a piece of wire around all 10 pieces of ribbon, and temporarily secure them together tightly. Check that this fits easily over your head. The ends of the ribbons should form a cascade down the front of the necklace. Note: You should have four lampworked beads in the top half of the necklace, and all other beads should be in the lower cascade. Adjust if necessary.

6. Cut a 10-in. (25cm) piece of 22-gauge wire, and string small chip beads, leaving about 1 in. (2.5cm) of wire at either end. Use beads in alternate colors. Wrap the wire around the temporary wire holding the ribbons together several times, and secure at the back by twisting the two ends together. Save ½ in. (1.3cm) of wire, and trim the excess. Wrap the wire and tuck it underneath the center piece. Remove temporary wire.

7. Make any necessary adjustments to make the necklace flow by moving the ribbons around within the centerpiece.

Tribal Princess

SKILL LEVEL ●●●

NECKLACE

Designed by Julie Snider, Jools by Julie
Lampwork by Cathy Lybarger

Run for the Roses
NECKLACE

Designed by Sarah Hendrix
Lampwork by Rebecca Jurgens

I was inspired to make this beaded necklace while watching majestic racehorses raise their heads to adoring crowds. Roses are draped proudly around their necks as the jockeys prance them around the winner's circle. It feels good to be a winner, so give this project a try and drape your own spray of roses!

Daisy Chain

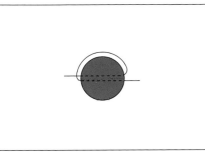

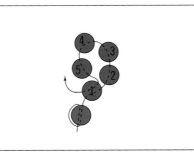

1. Thread a needle on 1½ yd. (1.35m) of black thread. String one bead and go back through, leaving at least a 6-in. (15cm) tail. This tension bead will help hold the piece together as you work.

2. To start the daisy chain, pick up five main-color seed beads. Go back through bead 1 in the opposite direction you went the first time to form a loop.

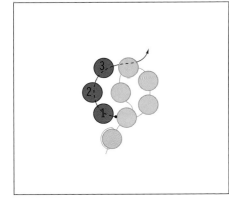

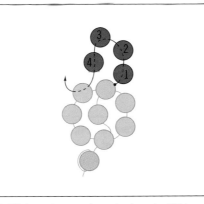

3. Pick up three main-color seed beads, slide them down to the loop, and then stitch back through bead 4 of the previous step. This will form your first daisy.

4. Pick up four main-color beads. Slide them down to the first daisy, and then stitch back through bead 3 of the last step.

HELPFUL HINTS

When working with seed beads, you do not need to see the holes. Dump a little pile of beads onto the cloth on your tray and just dip the needle through the pile. Then count the beads, if necessary.

Pinch the chain between your fingers to keep the tension tight. This will also determine the direction that the needle will travel. It will always travel to the *outside* of the chain.

THOUGHTS FROM THE DESIGNER —

I like combining colors and textures within a piece of bead-work. Shiny beads with matte beads make a wonderful combination. I love fringe. Nothing makes a piece unique like fringe. There is so much that you can do. It can be long, or short, simple or complex. It turns something simple into something extraordinary.

Supplies
Finished size: 23 in. (58cm) with fringe
Large lampworked focal bead
Seed beads
1 hank (60 grams) main color (black) seed beads
½ hank (30 grams) secondary color (matte iris green) seed beads
½ hank accent color (iris ruby) seed beads
100 10mm glass leaf beads
Nymo thread, 1 spool black size B and 1 spool off-white size B
Silver leaf clasp

Tools
Needles, size 12 sharp
Scissors
Chainnose pliers
Tray (either a cookie sheet or a plastic tray)
Fabric lining for tray so beads do not roll around

Sleigh Bells
NECKLACE

What's more fun than drinking hot chocolate and listening to the horse whinny as you travel through the woods on a wintry sleigh ride? This necklace jingles with the sounds of tiny silver bells and glistens with a rainbow of ice crystals. You don't need to live in the cold to enjoy this necklace. It is a must for every Snow Queen's winter wardrobe!

Designed by Sue Hart
Lampwork by Karen Leonardo

1. Cut a 20-in. (51cm) length of beading wire, and string a crimp bead, seven 2mm silver beads, and one half of the clasp. Go back through the crimp so the seven silver beads form a loop around the clasp. Crimp the crimp bead (Basics).

HELPFUL HINT

Keep all of the different items in separate piles. You can locate them quickly, and you won't use the wrong component by mistake. This is especially helpful with the crystals, since the colors are so similar.

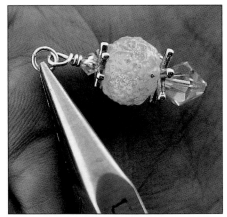

3. On a 2-in. (5cm) head pin, string an 8mm clear crystal, a 13mm silver snowflake bead, a small snowball bead, a 10mm silver snowflake bead, and a 4mm clear crystal. Make the first half of a wrapped loop above the beads. String the soldered jump ring, and complete the wraps.

2. String six rondelles, an opaque 4mm crystal, a small snowball, a clear 4mm crystal, a small snowball, an opaque 4mm crystal, a rondelle, an opaque 4mm crystal, a small snowball, a clear 4mm crystal, a small snowball, and an opaque 4mm crystal. String a rondelle, an opaque 4mm crystal, a large snowball, a clear 4mm crystal, a rondelle, a clear 4mm crystal, a large snowball, an opaque 4mm crystal, a small silver tube bead, two bells, an opaque 4mm crystal, and a large snowball. String a clear 4mm crystal, a rondelle, a clear 4mm crystal, a large snowball, a clear 4mm crystal, a tube bead, two bells, a clear 4mm crystal, a small snowball, a 13mm snowflake spacer, a clear 8mm crystal, a tube bead, and a bell.

4. String the focal charm, and then string the remaining beads, reversing the order from step 3. Thread on the remaining crimp bead and seven 2mm round beads. Pull the wire through the loop on the remaining clasp half and back through the crimp bead and the crystal rondelles. Using your pliers, pull the wire tight so there is no slack. Firmly crimp the crimp bead with your chainnose pliers to secure, and trim excess wire.

5. Give your necklace a little shake—just hear it jingle!

THOUGHTS FROM THE DESIGNER—

When I saw these fabulous beads, I immediately thought of winter and wanted to design a necklace that could be worn by the snow queen in Narnia. Anyone who has seen *The Chronicles of Narnia* will know what I mean.

Supplies
Finished size: 16 in. (41cm) choker
11 small lampworked snowball beads
8 large lampworked snowball beads
20 crystal rondelles, approx. 7 x 3mm
14 4mm bicone crystals, opaque white AB
17 4mm bicone crystals, clear AB
3 8mm bicone crystals, clear AB
Flexible beading wire, .018 or .019
12mm hammered silver toggle
10 5mm silver bells (they should tinkle)
14 2mm round silver beads
5 small tube beads, 5mm long (be sure the rings on the bells can thread onto these)
3 13mm silver snowflake spacer beads
10mm silver snowflake spacer bead
2-in. (5cm) 22-gauge head pin
4mm soldered jump ring
2 2mm crimp beads

Tools
Roundnose pliers
Chainnose pliers
Wire cutters

Snowflake Dazzle
RING

SKILL ●●○ LEVEL

Bold, flashy cluster rings are not for the faint of heart, and this one is no exception. Go for simplicity—complement the lampworked bead instead of overpowering it. The sparkle of the Swarovski crystals and the natural appeal of freshwater pearls in all shapes and colors make this ring a sparkly sensation!

Designed by Lisa Liddy, Joolz by Lisa
Lampwork by Karen Wojcinski

HELPFUL HINT

Always have more elements for these rings than you may use, because head pin ends can break off while you are wiring the element to the ring or you may want to move components once you begin.

1. Make sure the loop end of the ring form fits into the center hole of the disc bead. If it is too large, squeeze it gently with the roundnose pliers to fit. Place the disc bead over the loop, and thread a split ring through the loop, securing the disc bead on the ring form and providing a base for the dangles.

2. Assemble the dangle elements by threading the head pins with some of the daisy spacers and a pearl, silver charm, or crystal. Use your imagination and have a few extra ready to go. If you have decorative head pins (as shown in the picture), they can be used as is to fill gaps.

HELPFUL HINT

Some ring forms will fit with enough room for you to add the dangles without using the split ring. It will depend on the thickness of the disc bead.

THOUGHTS FROM THE DESIGNER —

I love making cluster-style rings. Making each ring is like putting together a puzzle that has no right answer. Each one is unique and eye-catching. The way the dangles fit and sit next to each other is flexible; the key is knowing when enough is enough.

Supplies
25–35mm disc-style lampworked bead in the shape of a snowflake
Sterling silver ring base
5mm split ring
10mm crystal cube, dark pink
2 8mm crystal rounds, light pink and alabaster pink
2 10–12mm silver butterfly beads
2 4mm crystal bicones, light pink
3 6mm crystal bicones in fuchsia, alabaster pink, and clear
8mm Czech tulip bead
3 8–10mm button pearls
5mm silver rondelle
Hill Tribe silver flower bead cap
2 decorative head pins
14 2-in. (5cm) head pins
8 3–4mm silver daisy spacers

Tools
Roundnose pliers
Chainnose pliers
Wire cutters
Crimping pliers
Design board

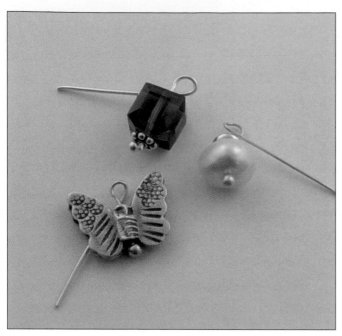

3. Make the first half of a wrapped loop (Basics) on each head-pin dangle so that you can have them ready to pick up as you assemble the ring.

4. Add one of the larger head-pin dangles to the split ring. Make a wrapped loop, and trim any excess wire, being careful not to cut the loop. Continue adding larger dangles to the split ring as desired.

5. After you have seven or eight head-pin dangles looped onto the split ring, the design will take shape. Add smaller dangles to fill in gaps and limit movement. The fuller the ring gets, the more difficult you will find the wrapping to be. Take care not to force anything.

6. Try the ring on and see how it looks. If necessary, remove a dangle and place it elsewhere by cutting the loop carefully and unthreading it.

Crisp Winter Days
NECKLACE

The organic borosilicate lampworked beads have a chilled look, with the breezy blue-gray base and a touch of the glowing red sun. The inspiration for this necklace was the bare branches of the trees in winter and the deep blue of the winter sky. It is a reminder of frosted sunny winter days.

SKILL LEVEL

Designed by Sue Hart
Lampwork by Bob Leonardo

Smoky Indigo
CHOKER

SKILL LEVEL ●●○

Designed by Julie Snider, Jools by Julie
Lampwork by Karen Wojcinski

Chokers are so "in" right now, and this one is fabulous with so many different components. The symmetrical design keeps the three strands clean and uncluttered. The lampwork is a rich, deep indigo blue dusted in metallics. Combined with smoky quartz and pink pearls, it's a real showstopper!

HELPFUL HINT
Adding an extension chain to your necklaces allows for more versatility if you're making a gift or an item for sale.

1. Sort your lampworked beads by size. Place the three largest beads in the middle of the center strand. Select the next four largest beads, two each on the top and bottom strand (seen in the photo as the seven center beads). Four discs are next, two top and two bottom; place the flattened beads next, two top and two bottom. Select the next four largest beads you have left; these go next to the flattened beads on the top and bottom. Select the next two largest beads; these go in the center strand on both sides of the focals. Use the last two beads as the last beads in the center strand.

2. Cut a 19-in. (48cm) piece of beading wire. Begin with the middle strand. String the lampworked focal, a ³⁄₈-in. (1cm) bead cap, a potato pearl, a ³⁄₈-in. bead cap, a lampworked focal, an 8mm bead cap, a potato pearl, a 6mm bead cap, a faceted oval quartz, a 6mm bead cap, a lampworked bead, a 6mm bead cap, a faceted oval quartz, a 6mm bead cap, a potato pearl, an 8mm bead cap, and a lampworked bead. String an 8mm bead cap, a 7mm mauve pearl, a 5mm spacer, a square faceted quartz, a 5mm spacer, a 7mm pearl, a 5mm spacer, a square faceted quartz, a 5mm spacer, a 7mm pearl, a 5mm spacer, a square faceted quartz, a 5mm spacer, a 7mm pearl, a 5mm spacer, a 4mm quartz round, a 5mm spacer, a 4mm pearl, a 4mm spacer, a 4mm quartz round, a 4mm spacer, a 4mm pearl, a 4mm spacer, a 4mm quartz round, a 4mm spacer, and a 4mm quartz round.

Repeat on the other end of the strand, skipping the first lampworked focal.

Supplies
Finished size: 16 in. (41cm), extends to 18 in. (46 in.)
23 lampworked beads
   3 beads ⅝ in. (16mm) round
   4 beads ½ in. (13mm) round
   4 beads ½ in. flattened
   8 beads ⅜ in. (10mm)
   4 discs ½ in.
18 8mm smoky quartz squares
10 14 x 10 faceted smoky quartz ovals
4 8mm smoky quartz faceted rounds
8 6mm smoky quartz rounds
22 4mm smoky quartz rounds
26 7mm mauve pearls
13 4mm mauve pearls
17 5mm mauve potato pearls
4 ornate silver beads, ½ in.
4 ornate flat bead caps ⅜ in.
22 flat bead caps 8mm
28 bead caps 6mm
48 5mm daisy spacers
31 4mm daisy spacers
3-strand clasp
2 in. (5cm) curb chain
3 head pins
6 crimps
Flexible beading wire, .018 or .019

Tools
Roundnose pliers
Chainnose pliers
Wire cutters
Crimping pliers

3. String a crimp bead and the center ring of one clasp half. Go back through the crimp bead, snug the beads, and crimp (Basics). Repeat on the other end. This section is 15½ in. (38cm) long.

5. String a crimp bead and the bottom ring of one clasp half. Go back through the crimp bead, snug the beads, and crimp. Repeat on the other end. This section is 17 in. (43cm) long.

4. Cut a 19-in. (48cm) piece of beading wire. Start at the center of the strand and string: a 8mm faceted smoky quartz round, a 6mm bead cap, a 8mm bead cap, a lampworked bead, an 8mm bead cap, a potato pearl, a 6mm bead cap, a faceted oval quartz, a 6mm bead cap, a lampworked disc, a 6mm bead cap, an 8mm faceted smoky quartz round, a 6mm bead cap, a potato pearl, an 8mm bead cap, a lampworked bead, a large ornate sterling silver bead, a lampworked bead, an 8mm bead cap, a 7mm pearl, and a 5mm spacer.

String a square faceted smoky quartz, a 5mm spacer, a 7mm pearl, a 5mm spacer, a square faceted smoky quartz, a 5mm spacer, a 7mm pearl, a 5mm spacer, a square faceted smoky quartz, a 5mm spacer, a 7mm pearl, a 5mm spacer, a 6mm smoky quartz round, a 5mm spacer, a 7mm pearl, a 5mm spacer, a 6mm smoky quartz round, and a 5mm spacer.

String a 4mm pearl, a 4mm spacer, a 4mm smoky quartz round, a 4mm spacer, a 4mm pearl, a 4mm spacer, a 4mm smoky quartz round, a 4mm spacer, a 4mm pearl, a 4mm spacer, and a 4mm smoky quartz round.

Repeat on the other end of the strand, skipping the 6mm smoky quartz round and starting with a 6mm bead cap.

6. Cut a 19-in. (48cm) piece of beading wire. String a faceted 8mm smoky quartz round, a 6mm bead cap, an 8mm bead cap, a lampworked bead, an 8mm bead cap, a potato pearl, a 6mm bead cap, a faceted smoky quartz oval, a 6mm bead cap, a lampworked disc, a 6mm bead cap, a faceted smoky quartz oval, a 6mm bead cap, a potato pearl, an 8mm bead cap, a lampworked bead, an ornate sterling silver bead, a lampworked bead, and an 8mm bead cap.

String a 7mm pearl, a 5mm spacer, a faceted square smoky quartz, a 5mm spacer, a 7mm pearl, a 5mm spacer, a faceted square smoky quartz, a 5mm spacer, a 7mm pearl, a 5mm spacer, a faceted square smoky quartz, a 4mm spacer, a 4mm pearl, a 4mm spacer, a 4mm smoky quartz round, a 4mm spacer, a 4mm pearl, a 4mm spacer, and a 4mm smoky quartz round.

Repeat on the other end of the strand, starting with the 6mm smoky quartz round and starting with a 6mm bead cap.

7. String a crimp bead and the top ring of one clasp half. Go back through the crimp bead, snug the beads, and crimp. Repeat on the other end. This section is 13 in. (33cm) long.

8. Add a silver extension chain to the ring end of the clasp. String combinations of pearls and spacers on three head pins to make accent drops. Attach the drops to the end of the chain with wrapped loops.

The Classics are, well, the Classics. This jewelry collection can be worn year-round, whether it is spring, summer, autumn, or winter. Classic jewelry pieces are usually neutral in color, or black and white, but not always. They are chic, refined, and elegant; they show sophistication and say you are a person of taste. The Classics never go out of style, so they can be worn for years to come.

Beads by Elise Strauss

Black & White Opera
EARRINGS

The Black & White Opera Earrings are perfect for day or evening. The earrings were originally inspired by the opera production *Don Giovanni*. The elegant "Drip Series" lampworked beads are large and make a dramatic statement with very simple beads. The overall impact of the jewelry design along with the unique style of the beads makes you want to stay for the grand finale.

SKILL
LEVEL

Design and lampwork by Darlene Durrwachter-Rushing

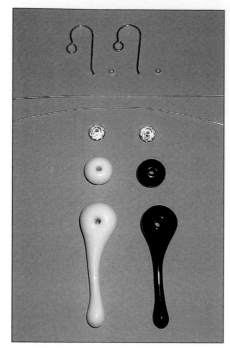

1. Tightly close the loops of the ear wires (Basics).

2. Thread a 6-in. (15cm) piece of beading wire through a lampworked drip bead.

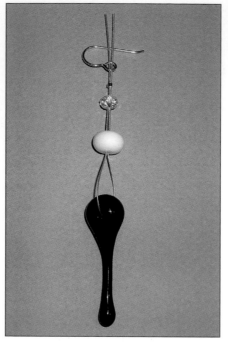

3. Thread both wire ends through a round lampworked bead, followed by a crystal rondelle, a crimp bead, and an ear wire.

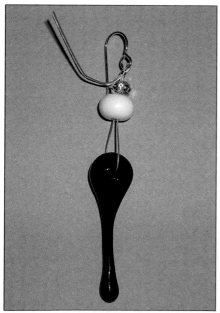

4. Slide the round lampworked bead and crystal bead down the bead wire, close to the drip bead. Fold ¾ in. (1.9cm) of both strands of bead wire over the ear wire loop, and string both strands back through the crimp bead. Crimp with crimping pliers (Basics). Trim wire ends right next to the crimp. Be careful not to cut the two bead wires threaded through your beads!

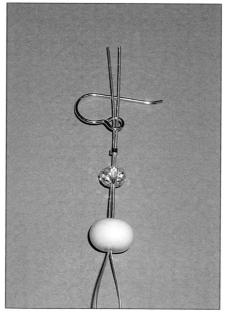

5. Repeat steps 2–4 with the remaining beads for the second earring. Match the placement of the components and length of the earrings to have evenly sized earrings. Make any adjustments needed for the earrings to hang properly. If your bead and ear wire need to be straightened to hang correctly, use chain-nose pliers and grasp the crimp bead, twisting gently with your other hand to center your bead with the ear wire as desired.

THOUGHTS FROM THE DESIGNER —

There is a permanency about glass beads that draws me to the medium. The beads I make will, most likely, last longer than I do. I love to imagine someone discovering one of my pieces of jewelry at some point in the distant future—it's my little nod to immortality. There is also a mystical, sacred element to beads: as amulets to ward off evil and invite good, as talismans, as manifestations of faith, as message-bearers, and as simple expressions of adornment. It's those many layers of expression and the deep sense of history in the making and wearing of beads that keeps me connected to this art form.

Supplies
Finished size: 3 in. (7.6cm) drop earrings
2 round lampworked beads, 1 black and 1 white
2 drip lampworked beads (hole at the top of the design), 1 black and 1 white
Flexible silver-plated beading wire, .018
2 6mm clear crystal rondelles
2 silver crimp beads
2 silver ear wires

Tools
Chainnose pliers
Crimping pliers
Wire cutters

Coco Elegance
NECKLACE

SKILL
LEVEL
● ● ○

This signature necklace style is inspired by the designer Coco Chanel. She believed in the tiny details of design and the total concept of wearability. Today's woman must exude confidence and self assurance, projecting to the world that she dominates her field. She tosses aside the trappings of a male-dominated world and dons an important necklace: one that frames her face, underlines her self-confidence, and draws her audience to her.

Designed by Teri Sallwasser
Lampwork by Karen Leonardo

HELPFUL HINT

When designing a unique necklace like this, choose beads with a variety of shapes and patterns to add more interest to your design.

1. Cut a 24-in. (61cm) piece of beading wire. String a crimp bead and a 6mm soldered jump ring, and go back through the crimp bead. Crimp the crimp bead (Basics). Trim excess wire close to the crimp.

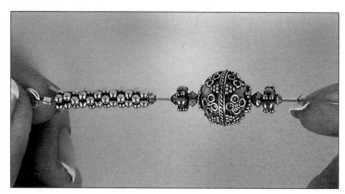

2. String twelve 5 x 3mm square beaded rondelles, a 3mm crystal bicone, a 3mm liquid silver tube, a 3mm crystal bicone, a 7 x 2.5mm spacer, a 3mm crystal bicone, a 14mm round, a 3mm crystal bicone, a 7 x 2.5mm spacer, a 3mm crystal bicone, a 3mm liquid silver tube, and a 3mm crystal bicone.

HELPFUL HINT

When stringing a large hollow bead on wire, it can be hard to find the hole coming out the back end. Look through the holes of the bead with a white sheet of paper as a background. Watch the end of the wire as it goes through the bead and exits the bead on the far side.

3. String a 10 x 8.5mm square bicone sterling bead, a 4mm crystal bicone, an 8 x 5mm spacer, a 4mm crystal bicone, a 12mm bead cap, a lampworked hollow, a 12mm bead cap, a 3mm crystal bicone, a dangle bead (sterling spacer with loop for dangles), a 3mm crystal bicone, a 20mm round, a 3mm crystal bicone, a dangle bead, a 3mm crystal bicone, a 12mm bead cap, a lampworked hollow, a 12mm bead cap, a 3mm crystal bicone, a dangle bead, and a 3mm crystal bicone.

4. String a bead cap, the largest (focal) lampworked hollow, and another bead cap.

5. Repeat steps 3 and 2 in reverse order to string the other half of your necklace.

6. String a crimp bead and a soldered jump ring, and go back through the crimp bead. Crimp the crimp bead. Trim any excess wire.

7. On each side, attach half of a clasp with a jump ring (Basics).

8. On a head pin, string a 7 x 2.5mm spacer and a 3mm crystal bicone; make six. On a head pin, string an 8mm crystal helix; make six. On a head pin, string an 8mm silver round and a 3mm crystal bicone; make six. Connect one of each dangle type to a loop bead's loop with wrapped loops (Basics), placing the crystal helix dangle in the center. Repeat with the remaining dangles and loop beads.

THOUGHTS FROM THE DESIGNER —

I love making bold jewelry for self-assured women, combining balance, movement, and color that accentuates but doesn't distract. Balance provides a perfect look, comfort, and wearability. Movement ensures that the wearer will be seen. My favorite jewelry is what I call the "power necklace," a feminine alternative to a man's power tie. This necklace gets noticed yet drapes comfortably on the neck.

Supplies
Finished size: 15¹/₂ in. (39.4cm) necklace, without clasp
- **5 lampworked hollow beads, about 18 x 23mm**
- **10** 12mm sterling bead caps
- **2** 20mm ornate sterling round beads
- **2** 10 x 8.5mm square bicones
- **2** 14mm round silver beads
- **6** round beads with loop for dangles
- **4** 7 x 2.5mm spacers
- **2** 8 x 5mm spacers
- **24** 5 x 3mm square beaded rondelles
- **4** 3.5 x 1mm liquid silver tubes
- Flexible beading wire, .018 or .019
- **2** 2 x 2mm "heavy wall" crimp beads
- **20** 3mm crystal bicones, crystal
- **8** 4mm crystal bicones, crystal
- Bar clasp
- **4** 6mm soldered jump rings
- **6** 7 x 2.5mm spacers
- **6** 8mm crystal helix beads, crystal
- **6** 8mm silver round beads
- **12** 3mm crystal bicones, crystal
- **18** 1¹/₂-in. (3.8cm) ball-end head pins

Tools
Roundnose pliers
Chainnose pliers
Crimping pliers
Wire cutters

Royal Kimono
NECKLACE
and EARRINGS

SKILL LEVEL ●○○

Designed by Bobbi Jansky
Lampwork by Joy Knepp

This jewelry is reminiscent of a royal kimono decorated with Chinese calligraphy. The design has a timeless classic line, with lots of color and texture. Chinese art is the theme: See how the necklace set shows the passion of Eastern art, the technical quality of the simplistic design, and the tranquility of the pieces produced during the Ming dynasty era.

Necklace

1. Cut a piece of flexible beading wire to your desired length plus about 6 in. (15cm). String a crimp bead and the clasp. Go back through the crimp bead, and pull the beading wire tight, leaving about a ¾-in. (1.9cm) tail. Flatten the crimp bead (Basics).

2. String the gold-filled saucer bead. Make sure it slides over the wire tail. Snip off the extra beading wire as close to the saucer bead as you can.

3. String three 16mm round onyx beads on the wire.

4. String a 12mm bead cap, a 16mm round onyx bead, and a 12mm bead cap.

5. String three 16mm round onyx beads.

6. String a fiber optic bead, a saucer bead, a 14mm lampworked bead, a saucer bead, and a fiber optic bead.

7. Add a 12mm wire bead cap, a 16mm round onyx bead, and a 12mm wire bead cap.

THOUGHTS FROM THE DESIGNER —

These lampworked beads are usually stunning on their own. My job as a designer is to highlight the work that has been carefully done in these artistic glass beads!

Supplies
Finished size: 18 in. (46cm) necklace
18 x 25mm focal lampworked oval
2 15mm lampworked bead
4 14mm lampworked bead
2 12mm lampworked bead
3 2½ in. (6.4cm) decorative gold head pins
2 2mm crimp beads
2½ in. (6.4cm) link chain (must fit through lampworked bead)
3½ in. (8.9cm) gold-filled chain (must fit through lampworked bead)
3 in. (7.6cm) open-link chain for extender
12mm gold-filled lobster clasp with attached jump ring
17 fluted saucer gold-filled beads
10 12mm wire bead caps
3 10mm wire bead caps
16 16mm round faceted onyx beads
6 10.5mm faceted onyx rondelles
4 8mm round faceted navy-blue fiber optic beads
4 10.5mm red glass rondelles
Barrel faceted onyx bead
Pair ear wires
Flexible beading wire, .018 or .019

Tools
Chainnose pliers
Roundnose pliers
Wire cutters

8. Add a 10.5mm onyx rondelle, a 10.5mm red rondelle, a saucer bead, a 15mm lampworked bead, a saucer bead, a 10.5mm red glass rondelle, a 10.5mm onyx rondelle, and a saucer bead (not shown).

9. String an end link of the 3½ in. (8.9cm) length of curb chain next to the saucer bead. String an end link of 2½ in. (6.4cm) chain. String a 12mm bead cap, a lampworked oval, and a 12mm bead cap (as shown in step 10 photo).

10. String a 14mm lampworked bead on the 2½-in. chain. Keep the chain straight; don't let it twist, or the dangles will not hang properly at the center. String the end link of the 2½-in. chain onto the beading wire next to wire bead cap. Repeat this step with the 3½-in. piece of chain.

11. Repeat the patterns in reverse from steps 8, 7, 6, 5, 4, and 3.

12. String a crimp bead and the 3-in. (7.6cm) section of bigger loop chain. Go back through the crimp bead, tighten the wire, and flatten the crimp.

13. String a gold saucer bead, an onyx barrel bead, and a 10mm bead cap on a head pin. Attach the dangle to the chain with a wrapped loop (Basics).

Earrings

1. String a saucer bead, a 12mm lampworked bead, a 10mm bead cap, a 10.5mm onyx rondelle, and a saucer bead on a head pin. Make a wrapped loop.

2. Attach an ear wire to the wrapped loop. Make a second earring to match the first.

Wildly Sophisticated
BANGLE

SKILL LEVEL ●●○

This animal-print bangle was inspired by an African safari. African women would be proud to wear this bangle with zebra, giraffe, and spotted lampworked beads. African wealth is shown through jewelry—the more baubles on the wrist, the more money the family has. Adorn yourself with this bangle, and you will have a jewelry piece ready for a wilderness adventure.

Design and lampwork by Christine Schneider

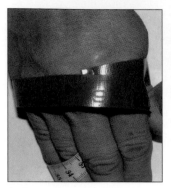

1. First measure tightly around the widest part of your hand (have someone help you). Take this measurement and add 1 in. (2.5cm). My measurement was 8½ in. (21.6cm) plus 1 in. (2.5cm) to equal 9½ in. (23cm). Divide this number by three. Round this number up to the nearest quarter inch. (My working measurement is 3¼ in./8.3cm.)

2. Cut a piece of wire to the length of your measurement. Make a simple loop on one end (Basics). This is where the curve of the wire is important. The opening of the ring will be on the uphill side of the curve. Repeat to make a total of 15 wires.

3. Randomly bead each piece of wire until there is ½ in. (1.3cm) of wire left on the end. Make a simple loop on the end. There are three sections of five wires each to the finished bracelet, so be sure that the wires of each section are unique and that the larger beads are spread throughout the wires. Try to achieve a random look.

HELPFUL HINT

The wire has a natural arch. Be sure that you pay attention to the curve while making the project. This arch will wrap around your wrist. If you try to work against the curve, the bracelet won't lie flat.

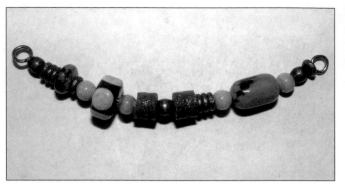

4. Take one wire from each section you have created. Use a split ring to connect the two end loops together: Open the split ring carefully, as you would a mini key chain ring. Keep the curve of the wires in the same direction. Make five individual bangles.

5. Hold two bangles over your fingers with the rings lined up. Use a jump ring to connect the two split rings together. Turn the bangles and repeat to connect all five bangles together.

6. Cut a 3-in. (7.6cm) length of wire. Make a simple loop, and string a small turquoise bead, a long lampworked bead, and a small turquoise bead. Make a simple loop above the top bead. Make three long bead units.

7. Slip a jump ring through the loop on the end of a long bead unit and through the split ring on one of the outside links of the bracelet; close. Repeat with the other long bead units and outside links.

8. Create three zebra dangles: String a small ivory glass bead, a washer bead, a zebra lampworked bead, a blue sand bead, and a round brass bead on a 2-in. (5cm) head pin. Make the first half of a wrapped loop (Basics).

9. Attach a zebra dangle to the outside split ring on the bracelet. Be sure this is on the outside of the ring so that it hangs away from the bracelet. Complete the wraps. Repeat, placing the dangles around the bracelet where the long beads meet, one in each ring section.

10. Make six more small dangles by stringing the remaining beads on head pins. Attach these in the same way as the zebra dangles, using wrapped loops. Attach one small dangle on each side of a zebra dangle, so there are three dangles on the outside of each jump ring section.

THOUGHTS FROM THE DESIGNER —

My designs are actually very simple to execute, even though they look complex. I like to layer my work, which means that I can stop at most any point in the design and have a great piece of jewelry. This simple three-link bracelet is great by itself. But if you make five of those bangles and link them together, you can create a more complex design. Add a long bead over those links, and it becomes ornate. Finally, attach some dangles to get the final design. You can stop after each new layer, if you like. Make what you love and embellish it until you are happy. If you create your jewelry this way, you will always love what you have made.

Supplies
Finished size: 7–8 in. (18–20cm)
3 lentil-shaped zebra lampworked beads
3 elongated giraffe lampworked beads
15 small spotted brown lampworked disc beads
15 4–7mm African turquoise barrels
23 4–7mm African turquoise discs
41 blue-sand cast-glass barrels
78 4mm ivory round glass beads
57 4mm round brass beads
134 4mm washer-style brass beads
5 ft. (1.52m) 20-gauge wire
9 2-in. (5cm) head pins
15 6mm split rings
18 6mm jump rings

Tools
Roundnose pliers
2 pairs of chainnose pliers
Wire cutters

LAMPWORK AND JEWELRY ARTISTS DIRECTORY

Lezlie Belanger
Canterbury Keepsakes
www.cankeep.com

Robin Bond
Lone Bird Designs
1201 West Toledo Court
Broken Arrow, OK 74012
www.lonebirddesigns.com

Susan Booth
2 Cats Designs
12 Wannon Court, Melton
South
Victoria, 3338
Australia
www.2cats.cjb.net

Kristan Child
Redside Designs
www.redsidedesigns.net

Amy Cornett
2470 Clairview St.
Alpharetta, GA 30004
www.amycornett.com

Shruti Gautam Dev
Artyzenworld
292, sector 15
Faridabad. Haryana
12007 India
www.artyzenworld.com

Darlene Durrwachter-Rushing
The Jelly Bean Machine
1239 Resaca Place
Pittsburgh, PA 15212
Drush68877@aol.com

Judi Emerman
Judibug Designs
2811 Belgrave
Pepper Pike, OH 44124
judibugdesigns@aol.com

Sue Hart
Bangles, Baubles, Beads
Flat 2, 36 Browning Ave
Bournemouth, Dorset
BH5 1NN
United Kingdom
www.baublesbanglesbeads.net

Sarah Hendrix
Shadowflame Designs
sbhbeadz@hotmail.com

JC Herrell
JC Herrell Glass
jc@jcherrell.com
www.jcherrell.com

Bobbi Jansky
8216 1st. St. SE
Everett, WA 98205
Ebay id: The Masters
Workshop

Lesley Jones
Bead Genie Creations
www.beadgeniecreations.com

Joanne Jovich
1083 Vista Pointe Circle
San Ramon, CA 94582
j.jovich@comcast.net

Rebecca Jurgens
L&S Arts
David & Rebecca Jurgens
Kingston, WA
www.landsart.com

Leslie Kaplan
Rush Creek Designs
125 S. Lang Ave.
Pittsburgh, PA 15208
rushcreek@verizon.net

Joy Knepp
1616 Short School Rd.
Somerset, PA 15501
jknepp@shol.com

Bob and Karen Leonardo
JustLeonardo/Leonardo
Lampwork
362 Hood School Rd.
Indiana, PA 15701
www.leonardolampwork.com or www.justleonardo.com

Lisa Liddy
Joolz by Lisa
4802 E. Ray Rd. #23-249
Phoenix, AZ 85044
www.joolzbylisa.com

Cathy Lybarger
Aardvark Art Glass
819 E. Johnson St.
Madison, WI 53703
www.aardvarkartglass.net

Cary Martin
15416 Greater Groves
Blvd.
Clermont, FL 34714
www.CaryMartinDesigns.com

Marilyn Martin
Into the Woods
425 Aderhold Rd.
Saxonburg, PA 16056
Intothewoodsdesigns@yahoo.com

Teri Sallwasser
301 Windmill Palm Ave.
Plantation, FL 33324
www.terisallwasser.com

Christine Schneider
Kiki Beads
419 Flager Rd.
Fort Collins, CO 80525
www.kikibead.com

Julie Snider
Jools by Julie
16194 Chalfont CR
Dallas, TX 75248
julieannsnider@aol.com

Elise Strauss
www.kiocreekbeads.com

Nicole Valentine-Rimmer
Victoria, BC Canada
www.NValentineStudio.etsy.com

Rickie Voges
237 Rangely Ct.
Simi Valley, CA 93065
rspv@aol.com

Vicki Wegener
2828 NE 32nd Ave.
Portland, OR 97212
victoriaperkinsstudio@yahoo.com

Karen Wojcinski
Wojobeada
367 Lake Shore Dr. W.
Dunkirk, NY 14048
kwojcinski@clake.org

DEDICATION AND ACKNOWLEDGMENTS

I dedicate this book to all the wonderful jewelry designers and collectors who use artist-made lampworked beads in their jewelry. I appreciate those who support Self-Representing Artists (SRA) beads and products, which helps us provide for our families and continue our obsession with hot glass beads!

I would like to thank my family (Bob, Brock, Erica, Braden, and G-ma Barb) for all the support and encouragement. I hope I make you proud! Special thanks go out to all the lampwork artists who make lampworking their life's passion. I appreciate all the support I have received from our local glass bead-maker's society, the 3 Rivers Glass Beadmakers (3RGB), through beads submitted for the book, and also all the encouragement with the development of my lampwork tools.

Thanks to the incredible lampworkers who created the beads appearing on these pages. A special thanks to Elise Strauss, who I met at the 2007 Gathering. She made the beautiful season beads in the chapter introductions.

Thank you to the very skilled jewelry designers who have expertly created the jewelry you see on these pages. Another special thanks to Lisa Liddy, who has helped me so much with getting the book organized and ready for the publisher.

Thank you to all those within Kalmbach Publishing who have helped in the editing, designing, illustrating, and photography for this book. Thanks to Erica Swanson, my editor for both of my books—you're very special! Also to Valerie Weber: You're so positive and encouraging—thank you. Thanks also to the photographers and artists who helped my book come alive.

ABOUT THE AUTHOR

Karen Leonardo has been a lampworker and jewelry designer since 1996, and she has authored and contributed to other lampworking and jewelry books. She has invented a glass tool called the Leonardo Petal Puller, which pulls petals from glass rods to be used in sculpted glass flowers. Karen also has a tool line called The Leonardo Imprinters; the tools imprint various designs into the hot glass.

Karen's accomplishments include honors in the art world as well as the business world. She is proud to have been nominated for awards, such as the Pennsylvania Artist of the Year and The International Who's Who of Business Women and Entrepreneurs. A member of the International Society of Glass Beadmakers, Karen runs a successful lampworking Web site with her beads, jewelry, books, and tools, and she is also an eBay power seller. Check out Karen's Web site, www.leonardolampwork.com, or look for her on eBay and etsy.